Has **Darwin** had his **Day**?

What the scientific journals say

DAVID ROSEVEAR

© 2007 David Rosevear

Published by Creation Science Movement

ISBN 978-0-9502090-7-4

Book design by Lisa Sodera at

onesmallmango.com

Photographs provided by CSM except where stated

Printing in Malaysia managed by
Bekaam Printers Pte Ltd.

Has **Darwin** had his **Day?**

What the scientific journals say

CONTENTS

Saturn NASA

FOREWORD

Let Hercules do what he may,
Yet every dog shall have his day.

It was a source of great merriment to learn recently that Charles Darwin, the father of modern evolutionary philosophy, is to have his very own day. Alas, poor chap; he will need more than a day. Already he has had nigh on the past 150 years to himself, and in that immense period of time he has had the finest brains in the scientific world fighting in his corner - often amongst themselves. Yet after all that effort, his theory of evolution is foundering today upon the rocks of observation and common sense. Indeed, there are those familiar with the parameters of scientific philosophy who would deny that his idea is a theory at all in the strict sense of the term. Beyond the realms of falsifiability, his idea is nothing more than a hypothesis, a hypothesis moreover that has failed every test put upon it.

Was there ever, in all the history of ideas, a comparable case of a man getting it wrong in such heroic proportions? One comes to mind, Ptolemy. He was the father of geocentricity, the idea that the earth stands still and all the heavens revolve around it. Yet Ptolemy did have one great advantage over Darwin. At least his theory of geocentricity was based firmly upon that most 'reliable' of scientific requirements, observation. The earth was not felt to move. It was not observed to move. To be brief, Ptolemy's theory met all the scientific criteria, not only of his own day, but of ours too. And that is the great irony of it. Ptolemy met every scientific criterion, and today he is laughed out of court. Darwin meets none, and is hailed as a scientific genius! It is the story of the emperor's new clothes all over again.

How does one correct such a situation? Well, perhaps it cannot be corrected, not entirely at any rate. All we can hope to do is add our own voices to that of the little boy who alone was aware of the fact that the emperor had no new clothes, and then hope that more will see the emptiness of the claim that indeed he has and very smart he looks too. This present book is one such voice. But it is not a lone voice in the wilderness. Rather, it echoes the voices of those whose job it is to support Darwin, to proclaim the genuineness of his suit of clothes, yet who are beginning to see through the myth, and whose honesty compels them to criticise their hero - sometimes wittingly, but sometimes unwittingly too. Moreover, the book has the advantage of being thoroughly up to date in its references, and that, sadly, seems to be a rare attribute these days. It is not meant to be merely a fireside read, but a working tool of study, and I would urge its readers to scrutinise it closely. For those already embroiled in the struggle, it will prove a most useful ally, whilst for those who are new to the controversy, it will be worth working through repeatedly. It is, in short, a gold mine, and I readily commend and endorse it.

Bill Cooper, PhD, ThD.

INTRODUCTION

Religion and Science

It is a truism that whereas for most of the first fifteen hundred years of the Christian era the official Church was regarded as the repository of all wisdom and authority, both sacred and secular, increasingly in the past five hundred years Science has usurped that position in the minds of most people in the West.

The reasons for this are two-fold. Firstly, the Church under the influence of men like Augustine and Thomas Aquinas espoused many false ideas of Greek philosophy. It also developed many false doctrines and practices, enhancing its own authority rather than the authority of Scripture. Following the merging of Church and State under Constantine the Great, the Church became increasingly a political as well as an ecclesiastical authority, and that influence was jealously guarded. When men like Copernicus and Galileo challenged the Greek idea that the earth was the centre of the Universe, the Church hierarchy and its thought police used their power to silence what they saw as a challenge to Church authority.

A second reason for the ascendancy of Science was that men such as Kepler and Newton, rather than simply following Greek cosmologies, began to discover the scientific laws that govern the natural world. The law of gravity pointed to a heliocentric system and the motion of the planets around a massive Sun at once dispensed with the epicycles of geocentrism. (With the subsequent detection of parallax in our observation of the nearby star Cygnus 1, the idea that the earth is the centre of the Universe finally became a lost cause to most people.) By observation, experimentation and deduction, the other sciences were now making rapid advances. Mendeleyev brought some order to the multiplicity of chemical elements with his Periodic Law. Boyle and Charles brought understanding of the behaviour of gases. Medical advances were made with the development of antiseptics and

8

anaesthetics, while Faraday broke fresh ground with his experiments in the modern science of electromagnetism. This new knowledge brought practical advantages to industry and everyday life. Science had established itself as the new authority.

Earth history rewritten

One new science, Geology, was derived from the development of canal navigation in the United Kingdom. Men such as Smith noted that there was an order to the types of rock sediments exposed by the 'navvies' in their excavations, as well as to the typical fossils they contained. Formerly it had been supposed that both the sediments and these relics of former life forms were the catastrophic result of a worldwide Flood in the days of Noah. But from the end of the eighteenth century, Hutton and then Lyell claimed that they had been laid down gradually over aeons of time. The 'scientific' view became that present day rates of erosion have always obtained. There had never been a worldwide catastrophe. The crust of the earth was therefore millions of years old. With the emergence of Hubble's Law in Astronomy, the distances to other galaxies were seen to be vast, and the light from them of great antiquity. Over the past two centuries our estimates of the age of the earth and Universe have been multiplied over and over again, from mere thousands to millions, and now to billions of years. Newton's and others' calculation of a six thousand year period of biblical history from the Creation was superseded. Scientific knowledge had seemingly triumphed over religious dogma.

The perceived long periods of earth history provided the time needed by Darwin for his theory of organic evolution, whereby it was proposed that all living things developed from one simple life form by gradual, slow processes. This was seen as the organising principle of biology. It was accorded the same scientific authority as the periodic table had to Chemistry, or the law of gravity to Astronomy. With scientific laws governing the whole of existence, organic life as well as rocks and stars, the need for a Creator was greatly diminished. A person could now offer scientific reasons for being an agnostic, or even an atheist. Anyway, if there was a powerful and good god, how could he allow the innocent to suffer in natural calamities?

With the undermining of the authority of the Bible and the Church came a need for a new basis for ethics. By what authority shalt thou not kill, commit adultery, steal or lie? Survival of the fittest had become the new order. Chance changes over long periods of time had replaced design as the causal mechanism.

Evolution theory questioned

But was evolution theory truly scientific, comparable with the principles of mathematics, physics and chemistry? With so much else involved apart from biology, we need to question this very carefully. Many modern scientists, including some within the life sciences, have expressed their doubts about Darwinism. With the continuing progress in knowledge of the life sciences, especially our new knowledge of genetics and bio-molecules, the short-comings of evolutionism are becoming more apparent.

In this little volume, we shall see what the experts in various scientific fields are saying. And because information is growing at an increasing pace, we have tried to use only recent quotations. The detail found in primary sources - the specialist journals where experimenters publish their findings - can be incomprehensible to the general reader. For this reason we will quote from review articles in general science journals such as *New Scientist* and *Nature*. These publications are used by scientists to keep abreast of important developments outside of their own specialist disciplines. Hopefully the general reader will be able to follow the discussions in the many disciplines from astronomy to zoology without being 'blinded by science'. Then by referring to these review articles in the library, the interested reader may use their references to find original papers if required. Rather than giving just references at the end of each chapter, we have quoted relevant passages within the text, as in the example below. This facilitates the flow for the reader.

Is the origin of the Universe a settled matter? Can we explain how life began without recourse to a Master Biochemist? Can mutations, acted upon by natural selection, account for the origin of species? Does the new science of genetics confirm our relationship to chimpanzees? What do the rocks teach us? Does everything point to chance or design?

> "But some people think that science is a kind of ultimate priesthood in itself and that it should be the ultimate religion and pay no attention whatsoever to God. That is a kind of fundamentalism of its own."
> John Templeton New Scientist, 17th September 2005 p. 46

CHAPTER 1

Where did the stars come from?

Speculations about origins

Science is not, of course, atheistic, but neutral, and scientists come in all shades of religious belief and unbelief. A Creator God would be beyond the reach of a measuring line, a weighing balance or a spectrometer. So science must seek explanations of a naturalistic kind. The existence of a super intelligent Creator cannot be ruled out by science as progress in science closes the gaps in our knowledge of the way things work. But discovering how living things function can tell us nothing about how they came into being. Naturalistic explanations of origins will by their nature always be speculative. Science deals with repeatable experiments, while such one-time-only events as the origin of the universe and the origin of life cannot be duplicated. Their study has to be in the realms of speculation and philosophy, rather than repeatable science. So what about the beginning of space and time, matter and energy? The ancients told tales of gods who wrought their magic in creating everything, while some Greeks thought that the whole lot had always existed without any beginning. The twentieth century Steady State Theory said much the same. The trouble with that thinking is that everything is seen to decay with time, and energy becomes less available to do work, so some kind of beginning becomes a necessity.

The Big Bang Theory is the story of origins currently favoured by most cosmologists. It proposes that in the dim and distant past (twelve thousand million years was one recent estimate, though it varies) there was nothing. This nothing became unstable and exploded. Space itself was made and expanded very rapidly. All of the matter in our Universe was present in that minute cosmic atom which then expanded out into a hot plasma of sub-atomic particles. Over time these particles cooled to the point where the simplest atoms, hydrogen, could form. Somehow gravitational forces overcame some of the kinetic energy of motion, and this hydrogen coalesced into stars and galaxies. The rest, as they say, is history.

There is, of course, some evidence that can be used to support such a scenario. When atoms are excited by heat, their electrons absorb and radiate quantities of energy that are peculiar to each kind of atom. This energy can be analysed by a spectrometer. The pattern of lines of the spectra is specific for any given atom. However, if one compares the spectral lines of, say, hydrogen in the laboratory with the hydrogen spectrum in a distant star or galaxy, one finds the self-same pattern but with their energies shifted to lower frequencies. This is called the red shift, and its value varies from star to star. It is thought that the size of the shift is a measure of the rate at which the star is speeding away from the observer on earth. Just as the frequency of a receding police car siren drops for a bystander on the pavement, so the red shift can be explained in terms of an expanding Universe. Everything is seen to be speeding away from everything else. So if time could be reversed we might find that everything did start out in the cosmic egg of the Big Bang theory. It has also been argued that those objects that are farthest from us are receding most rapidly. From this an estimate can be made of the age of the Universe. We shall return to this aspect when we discuss the age of everything.

A second line of evidence for the Big Bang theory is the discovery of a background radiation of just under three degrees above absolute zero temperature. It is the same in whatever direction one probes. This radiation had been predicted to be a consequence of the initial explosion of hot plasma, its energy red-shifted to the microwave region of the spectrum.

These two features supporting the Big Bang theory do not constitute proof of its reality, and other explanations of the phenomena may be proposed. For instance, the Soviet scientist Troitskii suggested in 1987 that both the red shift and the background radiation could be the result of a decrease in the speed at which light has been propagated since the beginning of time. This was not taken seriously at the time, but fresh evidence since the new millennium for a lowering of the speed of light with time puts this explanation back in contention. And should an expanding Universe be shown to be a reality (possibly necessary for dynamic stability) one cannot know how far back time goes. If the Big Bang theory is false and everything did not start at a point in space, then the universe may have been created only thousands of years ago in much the same state as it is today.

Difficulties with the Big Bang Theory
Something for nothing

But why should we want to doubt the reality of the Big Bang scenario? The problem is that there are several difficulties of a fundamental nature with the theory. To start with there is the conflict with the First law of Thermodynamics. This law states that matter and energy cannot be created by nothing, or destroyed. Many careful experiments have confirmed the truth of the laws of thermodynamics. Even in popular understanding, you cannot get something for nothing. 'Nothing' cannot create 'something'. If one appeals to a quantum perturbation of energy to produce the cosmic egg, one has then to explain the source of this energy. The astronomer David Darling voiced the difficulty as follows:

> "Don't let the cosmologists try to kid you on this one. They have not got a clue either – despite the fact that they are doing a pretty good job of convincing themselves and others that this is really not a problem …
> But there is a very real problem in explaining how it got started in the first place. You cannot fudge this by appealing to quantum mechanics. Either there is nothing to begin with, in which case there is no quantum vacuum, no pre-geometric dust, no time in which anything can happen, no physical laws that can effect a change from nothingness to somethingness; Or there was something, in which case that needs explaining."
> New Scientist, 14 September 1996, page 49

Order from an explosion

Another difficulty for the Big Bang theory is that there is so much order in our Solar System. We use the orderly progress of heavenly bodies to tell the time of day and to measure months and years. Order just does not come from an explosion, and the explosion of everything from nothing in a big bang should be the most chaotic event of which one can conceive. There would be no information at all in the subsequent arrangement of particles. The Second Law of Thermodynamics states that all spontaneous changes lead to a loss of order and information (an increase of entropy, that is, randomness). Energy alone, without information to direct it, cannot increase order. The proverbial bull in a china shop illustrates the difficulty of increasing order by undirected energy. These are just two of the problems for a naturalistic theory of the beginning of time, space, matter and energy. We shall encounter others in the detail.

Speculation

Much effort has been expended in calculating the timings of the stages in the possible progression from cosmic egg to stars and galaxies. The mathematics is one thing but the reality may be quite unrelated. No witness was there at the start, of course, so one can construct almost endless scenarios. There is more room for imaginative thinking in cosmogony than in other sciences. Here are a couple of quotes to support this view:

> "Scientists talk cheerfully and with immense confidence about the first few thousandths of a second of time, but secretly most people believe that they are making it up as they go along."
> The Guardian, 13 March 1997

> "Questions about origins have always held a strong fascination for the intellectually inclined, perhaps because such one-time-only events are difficult to study, so providing a vast playground for unbridled speculation and almost limitless armchair philosophy."
> Nature, 29 August 1996, p. 769

Missing Matter
Cold Dark Matter

A third major difficulty with the Big Bang theory is that following the explosion of everything, all the subatomic particles would fly apart at great speed, and would continue to separate by Newton's well tried laws of motion. How can these particles then coalesce to form atoms, molecules, nebulae, stars and galaxies? By what mechanism could they lose energy and cool down?

To solve this problem, cosmologists have invented an unseen form of matter to supply the gravitational force required to coalesce the particles. Because it cannot be detected, it is known as Cold Dark Matter, or CDM. It is calculated that to satisfy the demands of the theory CDM would have to comprise 95 to 99 per cent of the total matter in the Universe. Much effort has been spent hunting down this elusive material and much doubt has been cast on its existence, as the following quotes show:

> "Cosmologists have fitted their theoretical universes with some kind of invisible dark matter, to help galaxies to form …But for dark matter nor for inflation is there true independent support, outside the cosmological arena for which they were invented."
> Nature, 30 April 1992, p. 731

> "Nobody has yet detected any such dark matter particles so the case is still open."
> New Scientist, 29 Sept. 2001, p. 24

> "Like ghosts, dark galaxies may be a figment of the imagination. If so, our theories of how galaxies form are wrong, and we may have to change our ideas about what makes up most of the matter in the Universe, or rewrite the story of the Universe's first moments."
> New Scientist, 21 April 2001, p. 38

Where did the stars come from?

Explanations for the missing mass of the Universe border on the bizarre, which other scientists are not shy in criticising. Here are some examples taken from fairly recent scientific writings:

> CDM may be "wiggly lines of stringy stuff that stretches millions of kilometres across space, and super-heavy pretzel-like knots of energy"
> New Scientist, 27 Sept. 1997, p. 30

> And although the theory of superstrings is now causing great excitement in the physics community, there is to date not a shred of experimental or observational evidence to support it.
> Eric Chaisson, Cosmic Evolution, Harvard University Press, 2001, p.246.

> "99% of the mass of the Universe is in the form of black holes, each the size of a double bed."
> M. Hawkins, Hunting down the Universe, 1997

> "Nobody has ever seen a black hole ... But never mind the lack of physical evidence – there are enough problems in black-hole theory itself to make their existence seem implausible to say the least ... and concludes that black holes are a bag of contradictions that don't make a good case for their own existence at all."
> New Scientist, 19 Jan. 2002, p. 27

> "Dark energy may not exist, according to an international team of astronomers who have used an X-ray satellite to count galaxy clusters in the early universe. If they are right, the expansion of the universe is not speeding up and the scientific community has been taken in by a huge cosmic mirage."
> New Scientist, 6th December 2003 p. 10

Antimatter

Yet another difficulty for the Big Bang idea is that matter can only be created from energy ($e=mc^2$). But when energy produces matter, an equal quantity of antimatter is also made. These proceed to annihilate each other to form the same quanta of energy. A big bang could not make matter alone.

> "When the universe was created in the big bang, matter and antimatter were present in equal quantities. But along the way, the antimatter seems to have disappeared."
> New Scientist, 14 August 2004, p.13

> "There must always have been more matter than antimatter in our Universe. If it weren't so, we wouldn't be here. Matter and antimatter would have annihilated each other, leaving only radiation. What caused this asymmetry is still unknown, but it was vital for our existence."
> New Scientist, 15 January 2000, p. 45

The First Star

Let us suppose for a moment that CDM is a reality. We can imagine that hydrogen atoms have formed and come together with the gravitational aid of CDM to form a cloud. How can this nebula condense into a star? The hydrogen from the imagined primordial explosion will need to cool down, and the only way to do that is to exchange energy with molecules capable of absorbing energy. But such molecules do not yet exist in this scenario.

Once the first generation of stars have been formed (despite the problem just outlined) it will be possible by a process of nuclear fusion for hydrogen to form helium. Then eventually heavier elements like carbon, nitrogen, oxygen and iron can be synthesised as the stars get old, collapse and explode as supernovae. It is thought that the heavy elements are then incorporated into the next generation of stars, such as our Sun, and their planets.

But the difficulties of forming the first stars remain, even given CDM to provide the attractive force. Moreover, none of these necessary first stars, composed solely of hydrogen, have ever been detected. All stars are found to contain helium and heavier elements. Here are some more pronouncements by experts in this field.

> "Star formation is shrouded in mystery. Generally speaking a star forms when a cloud of gas collapses under gravity. However, if the cloud is too hot, pressure will combat the effect of gravity and prevent the cloud from collapsing. So to form a star, the gas cloud must have a way of cooling down. This isn't as easy as it sounds. In today's Universe this is accomplished by a huge array of molecules which collide and radiate away the heat. However, the atoms necessary for making all but the simplest molecule – molecular hydrogen – have to be made inside stars. It is a chicken and egg situation."
> New Scientist, 7 Feb. 1998, pp. 26-30

> "The truth is that we don't understand star formation at a fundamental level."
> Abraham Loeb, Harvard Center for Astrophysics, quoted in New Scientist, 7 Feb. 1998, pp. 26-30

> "We have no direct evidence of how galaxies were formed, how the first stars formed without the help of the prior generations of stars, how galaxies evolved, whether they were formed from aggregations of smaller units or from sub-divisions of larger ones."
> John Mather, NASA's Goddard Space Flight Center in Greenbelt, Maryland, USA in New Scientist, 7 Feb. 1998, pp. 26-30

Fresh ideas called for

In consequence of the foregoing arguments, astronomer Dr Eric Lerner and 33 colleagues wrote a letter of protest to *New Scientist* in May 2004, complaining that funding was not made available to research alternatives to the big bang theory of the origin of the Universe. The letter highlighted some difficulties and shortcomings of big bang cosmology.

> "Big bang theory relies on a growing number of hypothetical entities - things that we have never observed. Inflation, dark

matter and dark energy are the most prominent. Without them, there would be fatal contradictions between the observations made by astronomers and the predictions of the big bang theory. In no other field of physics would this continual recourse to new hypothetical objects be accepted as a way of bridging the gap between theory and observation. It would, at the least, raise serious questions about the validity of the underlying theory."
"What's more, the big bang theory can boast of no quantitative predictions that have subsequently been validated by observation."
New Scientist, 22nd May 2004 p.20

Then in 2005 Lerner pursued his complaint:

"'This isn't science,' says Eric Lerner... 'Big bang predictions are consistently wrong and are being fixed after the event.' ... Take the most distant galaxies ever spotted, for example. According to the accepted view, when we observe ultra-distant galaxies we should see them in their youth, full of stars not long spawned from gas clouds. This is because light from these faraway galaxies has taken billions of years to reach us, and so the galaxies must appear as they were shortly after the big bang. But there is a problem. 'We don't see young galaxies,' says Lerner. 'We see old ones.' ...'They are pretty much the same range of stars as present-day galaxies.'"
New Scientist, 2nd July 2005, p. 30

The Solar Nebular Theory

So the Big Bang Theory cannot explain the formation of stars and galaxies. Closer to home, there are difficulties in formulating a naturalistic theory for the formation of our Solar System. The current thinking is that the Sun and its planetary system condensed from a revolving cloud of elements and molecules. This is known as the Solar Nebular Theory. But once more, the laws of physics do not allow the formation of the system as we observe it. The following quotations from the appropriate scientific literature illustrate the several problems involved.

Where did the stars come from?

> "Our Solar System was built from the dust of dead stars. It's an often repeated fact. But if you ask how this dust actually started to form planets, you might get an embarrassed silence."
> New Scientist, 29 Sept. 2001, p. 24

> "The first question is how partitioning of material was achieved, whereby 0.0014 of the total mass ended up with 0.995 of the total angular momentum." "Next we ask how the planets, or planetary cores, would form."
> Leading British astrophysicist Michael Woolfson, Physics World, May 1996

The Sun should be spinning hundreds of times faster than it does if the nebular theory of the formation of the Solar System were correct. Instead it is the planets that actually possess 99.5 per cent of the angular momentum, while being a mere 0.14 per cent of the total mass. The Sun is truly massive compared with even the largest planet, Jupiter.

The angle of inclination of the spin axis of the Sun does not correspond with the plane of the orbiting planets. Michael Woolfson finds this an inconsistency if the system had been formed from a cloud of material.

> "The final question, rarely considered, may be the most challenging. The spin axis of the Sun makes an angle of 7° to the normal to the mean plane of the Solar System – virtually defined by Jupiter's orbit. Even if the mass-angular momentum could be achieved, then how could this 7° inclination come about?"

Woolfson then concludes:

> "… The [Solar nebular] theory is beset with difficulties and in some respects appears to be definitely unsatisfactory."
> Michael Woolfson, Physics World, May 1996

If our Solar System had started out as a single spinning cloud that condensed to form the Sun and all its planets and their moons, then the isotopic ratios of the elements should be the same throughout. This is not found to be the case. The ratio of nitrogen isotopes of masses 15 to 14 on Jupiter is only two-thirds that on earth. Hence the two planets are unlikely to have been formed in a common nebula (see New Scientist, 9 June 2001, p. 17).

Age and size of the Universe according to Big Bang Theory

Everything in the Universe is moving away from everything else, if the interpretation of the red shift of spectral lines is correct. The greater the speed of recession of a galaxy from the observer on earth, the greater is the red shift. Edwin Hubble, an astronomer in the first half of the twentieth century, concluded that the furthest objects from us were receding with the highest velocities. The ratio of speed to distance we call the Hubble Constant.

$$\text{The Hubble Constant} = \frac{\text{Speed of recession of object}}{\text{Distance away of object}}$$

The reciprocal of the Hubble Constant is a measure of age, because distance divided by speed equals time. The speed is calculated from the red shift. Distances in astronomy are too great to be measured by trigonometry, so they must be estimated. The brightness of Cepheid stars is used to estimate distances, by assuming that all such have the same intrinsic brightness. However, the amount of dust in space is not well known and can vary from one area to another. This affects the apparent brightness of stars in an indeterminate way. Distances may be estimated using the value of the Hubble constant, but the Hubble constant is itself estimated from the distance. This is circular reasoning. Astronomers do not agree with one another about the value of this constant. In a television programme a number of astronomers were interviewed, and each was asked to give the value of the Hubble constant. The programme edited their responses into a single sequence to emphasise that each used a different numerical value. This means that distances are largely guesswork and consequently the age of the Universe is uncertain. Of course, if the Big Bang Theory is wrong, we have even less idea about how old everything is.

> "The pity is that while discordance persists, cosmologists will not know which way to turn on questions like the reality of the Big Bang."
> Editorial - More muddle over Hubble constant, Nature, 27 July 1995, p.291

> "At the moment astronomers have no way of judging distances accurately."
> New Scientist, 24 Nov. 2001, p. 5

A Young Universe?

There are a number of phenomena that suggest that the Universe and the Solar System are much younger than the figure accepted by big bang cosmology. We need to examine these also.

The spiral arms of galaxies would have become fully wound up in billions of years.

Short term comets return in their elliptical orbits around the Sun every hundred years or less. Each time they come near the Sun, solar wind evaporates some material from these dirty snowballs, and this is seen as a cometary tail pointing away from the Sun. Eventually the comets break up and evaporate, or spiral in to the massive planet Jupiter. One has to ask why such short term comets are still circulating if the Solar System is 4.6 thousand million years old, as cosmologists claim. The standard answer is that a cloud of comets known as Oort's Cloud exists out beyond where they can be detected, and every once in a while a comet is deflected into a solar orbit by some perturbation. Oort's Cloud was invented to explain away this problem of short term comets and there is, of course, no observational evidence of its existence.

In 1835 Gauss first measured the earth's magnetic field strength (the unit for which is the gauss). Since then it has been measured frequently, and it is found that its strength is decreasing exponentially. In fact, the earth's magnetic field strength is decaying with a half-life of only 1,400 years. That is to say, in 600AD its strength was double today's value and in 800BC it was four times today's strength. In 2,200BC it would have been eight times that strength, and in only ten thousand years into the past, its magnetic field strength would have been like a magnetic star – a molten globe unable to support life. How is such an observation squared with the billions of years required by the Big Bang Theory? Mars has a magnetic field $1/800^{th}$ the strength of earth's field while Ganymede, Jupiter's largest moon, has a similar magnetic field strength to earth. One should not confuse the direction of the earth's magnetism with the field strength. Examination of the magnetism in the rocks shows that there have been a number of reversals in the direction of earth's magnetic field. There was one situation where an igneous intrusion showed a reversal between its top and bottom. From Newton's laws of cooling it was estimated that the reversal occurred in the space of a couple of weeks. These series of reversals may all have happened within a short space of time during a period of catastrophic activity in earth history. There is both laboratory and field evidence that sedimentary layers can be laid down very rapidly, and need not require the millions of years that Charles Lyell sought. (We shall return to this subject in a later chapter.)

The planet Saturn is surrounded by rotating rings of rocky fragments. These thin rings are kept in place by orbiting moons. It seems a very fragile situation, and one must wonder whether the rings could have been stable for 4.6 billion years? Neptune's outer rings have been shown to be decaying.

> "The first complete images of Neptune's outer rings to be taken in over a decade show that some parts of them have dramatically deteriorated and one section is close to disappearing

altogether…if the trend continues, Liberte [one arc] will be gone in a century."
New Scientist, 26 March 2005, p. 21

"Mars is a small planet, a tenth the size of earth, and models suggested that it should have cooled into an inert, cold lump of rock during the 4.6 billion years since it formed. But earlier this year new data showed that the core of Mars is still molten."
New Scientist, 29th November 2003, p. 12

The solar wind is continuously blowing dust particles across space, but because of our atmosphere, seas and sea floor spreading, we would not expect the dust to accumulate on our own planet. However, since the Moon is devoid of these features, it was estimated that over billions of years, a layer of perhaps fifty-four feet of dust might hamper lunar exploration. In practice, that one small step for Man revealed half an inch of dust. Maybe the estimate of the rate of precipitation was wrong. Maybe, unhindered by an atmosphere, much of the dust (with its high nickel content) smashing on to the Moon simply melted into the surface. (Or just maybe those billions of years are the estimate that is wrong.)

We have noted that stars, like everything else, get old and lose their energy. They then collapse, and the implosion can cause a supernova explosion that can be seen as a very bright object for days or even months, gradually becoming dim. That kind of stellar process is rapid. Other decays are also fairly quick, taking thousands rather than millions of years. It is a matter of observation that the companion star to Sirius was a red giant 1,500 years ago, but is now a white dwarf.

Spiral arms of galaxies, short term comets, magnetic field decay, Saturn's rings, Moon dust and rapid stellar processes all suggest that the cosmos may be thousands rather than billions of years old. The contrary evidence from the Hubble constant is far from convincing. And consider this, if the speed of light has, like everything else, decayed with time, then light from distant stars would have reached the earth very quickly in the past.

If the naturalistic description of the origin of the Universe requires billions of years, if the Big Bang Theory is an inadequate picture, if star formation is a mystery, then the alternative is that the heavens were designed by a Master Cosmologist. One might imagine that the evidence for such a Creator was outside the scope of science, but in fact, science has a name for it – the Anthropic Principle.

The Anthropic Principle

The Anthropic Principle recognises that the fundamental constants of the Universe – the gravitational constant, the relative masses of protons and neutrons, and many other conditions are fine-tuned for the existence of life. Anthropos is the Greek word for man, and the name 'anthropic principle' derives from the idea that conditions in the Universe are just right for man. The simplest explanation is that a Master Designer created it all as a complete package.

If the proton were 0.2% heavier, there could be no hydrogen atoms, and therefore no stars. Hydrogen is also a major constituent of water and all biological molecules. How fortunate all round that the hydrogen nucleus, the proton, is stable relative to the neutron. Newton found that the force of attraction between two objects, their gravitational attraction, is directly proportional to the product of their masses and inversely proportional to the square of the distance separating them. If the gravity force were not precisely inversely proportional to the square of the distance, then the Universe would not hold together.

Other conditions are just right for life on earth. For example, the position of our Solar System in the galaxy is optimal. If we were near the middle of the Milky Way, the concentration of stars would give us no night, and radiation levels would be harmful. If we were at the edge, the night sky would have no features. Then again, the earth's orbit around the Sun is circular rather than elliptical. The variations in temperature with the seasons are mild. The distance of the earth from the Sun is ideal. If earth were 5% nearer the Sun the seas would boil and if we were just 1% further away they would freeze. Our daily rotation rate is ideal for temperature regulation and for sleep pattern. A much slower rate would lead to soaring temperatures during the daytime and freezing conditions at night.

> "I think … that our Sun is extraordinarily stable … We seem to have found a star that is extremely stable and friendly to life - or we are just on a star that happens to be stable right now and will not always be so.
> "Other stars emit super flairs from time to time that are 10,000 times more powerful than our Sun's emissions. Most other systems contain two or three stars with convoluted orbits about each other.
> "If we were 5% nearer the Sun the seas would boil; if 1% further away they would freeze."
> New Scientist, 9th January 1999, p. 15

Our own star, the Sun, is very special, as recognised by astronomers.

> "So what is so special about our Sun? Firstly it is a single star, whereas most stars are in multiple systems. Then again, the Sun has about a third of the variation in brightness found in most other stars."
> G. Gonzalez, University of Washington in Seattle, New Scientist, 26 June 1999, p. 17

The distance of the Moon from the Earth is also just right. Our Moon stirs up the seas, aerating the upper levels so that plankton can flourish. If the Moon were much closer, tides would wash over the continents and erode them away. Too far away and the seas would not be oxygenated to support the marine food chain. The Moon also provides a calendar visible from everywhere on earth. The proximity of our comparatively large Moon locks its motion to us so that we only ever see one side of it. This has the effect of stabilising the angle of inclination of the earth's axis to the plane of our orbit around the Sun, a phenomenon that provides our seasons.

Moon rise from space
NASA

Where did the stars come from?

> "The problem of the Moon's origin has perplexed astronomers for a great many years. All the numerous theories proposed have been found to suffer from serious flaws."
> New Scientist, 7th June 2003, p. 54

The massive planet Jupiter shields the earth from comet bombardment by attracting them as in the case of the Shoemaker-Levi 9 comet that disintegrated and crashed into Jupiter in July 1994.

The ground with its mineral structures and composition, the hydrosphere of rivers and seas and the atmosphere with its proportions of oxygen, nitrogen and carbon dioxide, are all exactly suited to support plant and animal life. So is this simply a happy series of coincidences that we can write off as chance? No, because the chance of each perfect situation must be multiplied by the odds of every other one, and the product becomes astronomical in both senses of the word.

> "Physicists calculate that the probability of our Universe having the ingredients of life purely by chance is about 1 in 10^{229}. To argue that mathematics alone can win us that miniscule chance is, in the end, no less mystical than invoking a divine creator. Mathematics becomes the creator."
> New Scientist, 24 May 1997, p. 39

Ten to the power 229 can be better appreciated if one considers that it is ten times as great as ten to the 228. It is estimated that there are some 10^{80} particles in the whole of the Universe. (The age given to the Universe by cosmologists is about fifteen thousand million years, and this great age is still less than 10^{18} seconds.) So the odds against our Universe being so ideal for Man are so great that the work of a Designer seems the only reasonable conclusion to come to. The alternative that our Universe is just one of about 10^{229} other Universes, and that we only know about our own because it is the one that got it right, seems more far-fetched than belief in a Creator. However, if your objection to a Creator is philosophical rather than scientific, you may stretch credibility to the point of gullibility. Dr. Michio Kaku of New York, author of *Hyperspace: a scientific odyssey through the 10ᵗʰ dimension*, OUP, 1995, suggests the following:

> In the beginning there was Nothing, which was unstable, began to decay, and boiled with billions of tiny bubbles forming, and each expanded into a Universe. Bubbles in Kaku's multiverse are joined by Wormholes connecting with black holes in each one. Our Universe is the one-in-a-billion which is fine-tuned for life.

(One in a billion should be one in 10^{229}!) According to Kaku, someone could slip through a wormhole and find themselves in an alternative Universe. Though to be fair to him, a lot of people do go missing every year.

Sir Fred Hoyle was one of those astronomers who were prepared to think the unthinkable. He recognised that the odds against chance were too great and wrote:

> "The picture of the Universe, and the formation of the galaxies and stars as it has unfolded in astronomy is curiously indefinite, like a landscape seen vaguely in a fog … A component has evidently been missing from cosmological studies, a component involving intelligent design."
>
> Astronomer Sir Fred Hoyle in his book *The Intelligent Universe*

It is estimated that the observable Universe contains 400,000,000,000 galaxies, each containing billions of stars. This number is comparable with the number of grains of sand on the seashore. At the time when the Bible makes that comparison (Genesis 22:17), telescopes had not been invented and only just a few thousand stars were visible to Abram.

> "There are 10 times more stars in the night sky than grains of sand in the world's deserts and beaches, scientists say."

Where did the stars come from?

"There are 70 thousand million million million - or 7 followed by 22 zeros - stars visible from the earth. The estimate is said to be the most accurate yet…Without a telescope it is possible to see around 5,000 stars from the darkest places of the earth."
Daily Telegraph, 23rd July 2003

The Hebrew prophet Isaiah was moved by the sight of the night sky to marvel at the greatness of the Designer.

Isaiah 40:26 "Lift up your eyes on high, and behold who has created these things, that brings out their hosts by number: He calls them all by names by the greatness of His might, for that He is strong in power; not one fails."

The Hubble Space Telescope took 12 days to take one photograph. "The result showed 10,000 galaxies sprinkled across an area of sky just a tenth the size of the full moon."
New Scientist, 20th March 2004, p. 14

David's Psalm 19 affirms that the heavens declare the glory of God the Creator. They are visible throughout the earth each night and day. His handiwork is self-evident and needs no words.

Psalm 19:1-6 "The heavens declare the glory of God; the skies proclaim the work of his hands. Day after day they pour forth speech; night after night they display knowledge. There is no speech or language where their voice is not heard. Their voice goes out into all the earth, their words to the end of the world."
"In them He has set a tabernacle for the sun, which is as a bridegroom coming out of his chamber, and rejoices as a strong man to run a race. His going forth is from the end of the heaven, and his circuit to the ends of it: and there is nothing hid from its heat."

Thus the Psalmist continues by identifying the God of Creation as the

Lord Jesus Christ, who has promised to come again to the earth in power and great glory.

> **Rev 21:3** Behold, the tabernacle of God is with men and He will dwell with them…

> **Malachi 4:2** But unto you that fear my name shall the Sun of righteousness arise with healing in His wings; …

> **Matthew 25:1** Then shall the kingdom of heaven be likened unto ten virgins, which took their lamps and went forth to meet the bridegroom.

> **Luke 11:21-2** (In the context of allegedly casting out spirits by the power of Satan:) When a strong man armed keeps his palace, his goods are in peace: But when a stronger than he shall come upon him, and overcome him, He takes from him all his armour wherein he trusted, and divides his spoils.

> **Matthew 24:27** For as the lightning comes out of the east, and shines even to the west; so shall also the coming of the Son of man be.

> **Matthew 24:30** And then…they shall see the Son of man coming in the clouds of heaven with power and great glory.

CHAPTER 2

How did Life commence?

Pasteurised Soup

The ancient Greeks believed in the spontaneous generation of life, and this idea persisted almost into modern times. After all, we know that lice develop in dirty old socks, and mice in stored grain. It was Louis Pasteur who finally laid to rest the idea that simple living things can grow from nothing. He boiled up some broth that contained proteins, fats and other components of organic tissue. When left to cool in the air it was not long before mould started to grow on the surface. But he found that by excluding the air no mould developed. The Campbell's Soup Company is forever grateful to Pasteur for discovering that it is air-borne bacteria that cause the mould. Life could not have arisen spontaneously from a primeval soup. Similarly, lice or mice simply moved in to sample the delights of old socks or grain. It is not possible to generate living things from non-living matter.

If the earth cooled down from a hot gaseous state, there would have been a time when life did not exist here. So how did life begin? Those who look for a naturalistic explanation must believe that at some stage non-living matter developed spontaneously into a very simple living, reproducing thing. For example, Richard Dawkins, that fervent apostle of Evolution Theory, said in a Channel 4 TV programme in September 1996:

> The first living cell arose and from that we all descended, be it plants or animals or humans. That's an established fact. They're all cousins. Scientists accept it. Not to believe it would be absurd.

Advances in molecular biology

Since the middle of the twentieth century, great advances have been made in biology at the molecular level. The genes with their information coded on to the nucleic acid DNA are strung together on the pairs of chromosomes, together with genetic signals that tell the genes when they should be active. The DNA (deoxyribonucleic acid) is made of two spiral parallel chains of nucleotides, each nucleotide consisting of a phosphate group and a sugar (deoxyribose) with a base molecule as a side group on the sugar.

(We may note in passing that the sugars can exist as stereo-isomers, but in the nucleic acids there are only right-handed sugars. These could not be made by chance; the living cell provides the template for the correct configuration. We may also note that the bonding of the phosphate groups across the sugar is not the thermodynamically stable configuration one might expect from a chance construction. That arrangement would not give a biologically active molecule.)

The two component chains of the DNA are joined by weak hydrogen bonds between the bases. There are four different bases, designated A, T, C and G from their initial letters. Such are their shapes that A will only pair with T and C with G. The genetic information is encrypted in the specific order of the bases on the string of nucleotides, just as the information on this page is encrypted in the order of the twenty-six letters of the alphabet. Three consecutive bases form a codon, so there are 4x4x4 = 64 different codons. These code for the twenty different amino acids and for starting and stopping a sequence in a protein. There is some redundancy so that some amino acids can be coded for by more than one codon. (Two bases rather than three would have given only 16 different codons, which would be insufficient.) The codons are transcribed onto sections of RNA (ribonucleic acid) that are single stranded. Various proteins cooperate with the RNA to produce the appropriate amino acids corresponding to the codons. The resulting string of amino acids forms the designed protein.

Notice that in the cell many specific proteins are required along with the genetic information in order to make a protein. How then could the first protein have been formed by chance? Each protein has a specific order of amino acids corresponding to the order of the codons that in turn follow the order of the bases on the DNA. There is nothing haphazard about this process.

We know how DNA is replicated when cells divide. The twisted double strands are held together by weak hydrogen bonds between bases. At cell division the two chains separate and each separate strand becomes a template to construct a copy of the opposite strand, so that one DNA molecule becomes two. This process requires the cooperation of a number of enzymes, proteins that catalyse the formation of DNA.

> "It is a classic chicken-and-egg problem. DNA codes for the proteins that catalyse the chemical reactions that replicate DNA. How could one exist before the other?"
> New Scientist, 4th September 2004 p. 24

We are learning more and more of the course of metabolic pathways whereby molecules in the cell undergo the most complex series of chemical reactions at normal temperature and pressure to enable a living cell to operate. We have increasing knowledge of the structure of enzymes and other macromolecules. Since all life has the same bio-molecules, similar genetic molecules and proteins, and comparable metabolic pathways, it is reasonable for Professor Dawkins to say that they are all related. But can we assume that they are related by common descent, or is it more reasonable to say that they are related by common design? We need to look at the evidence.

Spontaneous generation of life?

In the 1920s the Soviet scientist Oparin suggested that life may have started in some warm pond where phosphates and other minerals had become concentrated. Simple carbon compounds and dissolved ammonia might have been activated by electric storms and energized by ultraviolet light to produce the first very primitive, yet self-reproducing, life form. His ideas were taken up in the West by fellow communist Haldane. With very little knowledge of biochemistry at that time, the ideas seemed plausible. Then, in the early 1950s, Urey and Miller in America tried some simple organic chemistry experiments in the laboratory. They placed methane, ammonia and hydrogen in a flask of water with a condenser and cold trap and boiled them up together. They passed a high voltage current through the vapours to simulate a natural electric storm, and then irradiated it all with ultraviolet light. In the cold trap they isolated a tarry mess which was found to contain glycine and beta alanine, the two simplest amino acids. Proteins are composed of a string of amino acids, so hopes were raised that given enough time, large bio-molecules could arise by chance and organise themselves into a primitive cell.

In February 1991, forty years on from his experiment that had raised such hopes, Professor Miller was interviewed by the monthly journal *Scientific American*. Miller said that the problem of the origin of life had turned out to be much more difficult than he, or anyone else, had thought. So what had dashed the high hopes of his youth? As we have already mentioned, the second half of the twentieth century saw giant strides in our knowledge of biochemistry and genetics. The simplest cells are seen as incredibly complex. The information from genes on the DNA is transcribed to RNA. Then the proteins are made in ribosomes within the cell using the information now on the RNA, with the help of some one hundred other specialised protein molecules as mentioned above. Moreover, the DNA and RNA are also constructed with the aid of protein molecules. With such interdependence of genes and proteins, it seems that all parts of a cell must be present and working before anything can work. Proteins are needed to make nucleic acids, and nucleic acids are required to make proteins - a chicken and egg situation.

How did life commence?

> "It has long been thought that the first self-replicating organisms could not have used today's system of DNA and proteins because it is too complex and interdependent to have arisen spontaneously. DNA encodes the proteins that catalyse the chemical reactions that replicate DNA - one could not exist without the other."
>
> New Scientist, 3rd September 2005 p. 26 (see also quote on page 35)

Because the DNA-protein system is seen to be much too complex to have arrived by chance, it has been suggested that RNA might have been a simpler alternative. The single-stranded RNA has only limited enzymatic properties while still carrying information like DNA. However, RNA is also complex, and no primeval soup experiment has ever thrown up anything like RNA. Moreover, **RNA cannot replicate itself**, a prime necessity for a living cell. RNA's enzymatic properties are not sufficiently versatile to meet the requirements of even the simplest cell.

RNA, like DNA, contains genetic information. All of our experience tells us that information only originates from an intelligent source, and is corrupted by chance changes. The mechanism of Neo-Darwinian evolution is said to be natural selection acting on genetic mutations. Yet **the corrupting of precise genetic information can hardly lead to the increasing complexity required by evolution theory**. Where did the genetic information coded on nucleic acids come from? Information has meaning and purpose. This is quite the opposite of chance. Professor Werner Gitt has pointed out that as a carrier of information, DNA is 4.5×10^{13} times more efficient than the silicon mega-chip. The mega-chip was, of course, created by teams of designers. Chance changes were rigorously excluded from their processes.

> "It is the information content, or software, of the living cell that is the real mystery, not the hardware components."
>
> New Scientist, 18th September 1999 p. 24ff

Amino acids (with the exception of glycine, the simplest, which lacks chirality's left and right handedness) can exist as stereo-isomers, being left- and right-handed. However, in proteins only left-handed amino acids are found. When amino acids are made in Miller-type experiments, a fifty-fifty mixture of right- and left-handed molecules is made. These are of no use for making proteins since the right-handed ones spoil the required three dimensional shapes that is necessary for the protein to do its job in the cell. The order of amino acids in a protein is decided by the order of codons on the gene that codes for it. Just any old order of amino acids will not function. Since proteins are from hundreds to thousands of amino acids in length, getting the order right from a pool of twenty varieties of amino acids as found in nature, simply by chance, is quite beyond the realms of possibility. (The odds of getting a specific protein of 100 amino acids in length would be 20^{100}. This figure is far in excess of the total number of particles in the Universe.)

> "In Genesis and the Big Bang, Gerald L Schroeder states that to create a single protein by chance, 10^{110} trials would have had to be completed each second since the start of time ... These computations are a formidable barrier to accepting the chance formation of life."
> Scientific American, March 1995 p. 8

Could a primitive cell make do with a much smaller protein that would then gradually evolve to those of present day sizes? Proteins need to fold up into a three dimensional shape in order to function. The packing of the folded molecule is extremely tight, using van der Waals forces that only attract over a very short range, plus other types of bonds such as sulphur to sulphur covalent bonds (between two cysteine amino acids) as well as hydrogen bonds. Folding is only possible with a length of at least seventy amino acids, so there are no very short proteins that might conceivably turn up by chance. The folded protein has amino acids with hydrophobic (water repelling) side chains at the inside of the folded protein but with hydrophilic (water seeking) side chains on the outside. The shape and position of active groups gives the protein its specific properties as structural features or enzymes. The position of almost all of the amino acids in any protein is critical, not only in order to fold tightly, but to have the shape and active groups to bind to other macromolecules. Miller now rightly sees his experiment as of no biological significance.

Despite these difficulties, others have suggested that life might have evolved by chance at a mid-ocean ridge where hot water laden with chemicals wells up into the ocean. There are some anaerobic bacteria that can metabolise hydrogen sulphide and colonise these inhospitable regions. However, the same problems of the improbability of proteins and genes, as well as the need for everything to work together, apply to this scenario also. Another suggestion for the origin of life is extra-terrestrial seeding. It seems that if it happened far away and long ago anything is possible. Much speculation has surrounded the finding of minute shapes in a meteorite found in Antarctica and thought to have originated on the planet Mars. If the shapes were 'nano-fossils' (much smaller than any fossil bacteria found on earth) then Mars might have teemed with primitive life once upon a time. The *New Scientist* for 8th August 1998 reported that the meteorite 'nano-fossils' claim was deliberately hyped by NASA to obtain funding for a further Mars probe. The scientists got their Mars probes (a couple were launched in 2003) but it was finally shown that the minute shapes on the meteorite were not organic in origin.

The not-so-primitive cell

The complexity and specificity of the simplest living cell cannot be over-emphasised. The cell wall allows nutrients in but excludes toxic material. It allows waste products out but retains useful bio-chemicals. Eukaryotic cells, found in all plants and animals, have a nucleus bound within a semi-permeable membrane that holds all the pairs of chromosomes that contain genetic information. Outside of this nucleus the cell is criss-crossed by microtubules of the protein actin that not only gird the cell into shape but act as roadways for proteins such as kinosine to carry bio-chemicals from their place of production to where they are needed in the cell.

Then there are the many sorts of 'organelles'. Some use food to produce energy, others use RNA and proteins to manufacture proteins as required, and still others police the cell for illegal immigrants. Professor Lynn Margulis has suggested that primitive, simple proto-cells lacked these organelles, which however, existed independently of the cell. The simple proto-cell and the organelles cooperated by symbiosis. Finally, Margulis suggested the cell assimilated the vital organelles to become the complex structures we find today. However, these components cannot now exist independently, nor could the cell exist without them. Moreover, one organelle, a lysosome, contains enzymes that destroy foreign bodies, so there are several reasons for rejecting this speculation as to how a complex machine could be built up little by little. A cell cannot operate today unless it is complete, with all its interacting metabolic pathways, each one usually involving dozens of steps and the cooperation of dozens of enzymes.

Another type of organelle found in the cell are the mitochondria. These components are packed with folded membranes that contain large numbers of tiny motors called ATP synthase. As part of a multi-stage process the sugar glucose is oxidised and the energy released by the process captured as ATP (adenosine triphosphate). Among the products are hydrogen ions and these pass through the mitochondrial membranes and activate the motors. The job of the ATP synthase motors, as the name implies, is to synthesise ATP from ADP, its diphosphate. The vital motor ATP synthase is another of these improbable macromolecules. It contains a wheel that rotates at 6,000 rpm when just ticking over, and each revolution converts three molecules of ADP to ATP. When a person spends a lazy day he converts his own body weight of ADP into the triphosphate, ATP. The latter is used by a host of bodily reactions that require a source of energy to complete them (muscle contraction, heart beat, moving chemicals about the cell, etc.), and the ATP is in turn recycled as ADP and phosphate.

The motor, which is 200,000 times smaller than a pinhead, is composed of thirty-one protein molecules. It only works when all parts are complete. There could not be a simplified Mark 1 version. It is present in all bacteria, fungi, plants and animals, so this amazingly improbable macromolecule had to be complete in the earliest life forms.

Motor cars are quite complex and William Paley would certainly not have imagined that one could just happen without a team of designers. Now a plant for making motor cars is orders of magnitude more complex than its product. In the same way, the DNA, RNA and hosts of proteins used to assemble the ATP synthase motor are together far more complex than even that improbable macromolecule. And the information required to make all of this work leaves one speechless with admiration.

A lost cause?

The components of a cell cannot work unless all of its parts are operative. Nothing works unless everything works. It is small wonder that many who have worked in this field of the origin of life have been forced to admit that they are no nearer a solution than Urey and Miller were in the mid 20th century. Sir Fred Hoyle writes that the probability of life forming from inanimate matter:

> "is one to a number with 40,000 noughts after it … It is big enough to bury Darwin and the whole theory of evolution. There was no primeval soup, neither on this planet nor on any other, and if the beginnings of life were not random, they must therefore have been the product of purposeful intelligence."
> Nature, 12th November 1981 p. 148

> "One must conclude that, contrary to the established and current wisdom a scenario describing the genesis of life on earth by chance and natural causes which can be accepted on the basis of fact and not faith has not yet been written."
> H P Yockey, Journal of Theoretical Biology, vol 67, 1977 p396

"There is nothing in the known laws of nature that says life is inevitable."
"Biochemists have inched forward in their attempts to synthesise the building blocks of life, but creating life in a test tube remains a distant dream."
New Scientist, 18th September 1999 p. 24ff

"Nobody knows how a mixture of lifeless chemicals spontaneously organized themselves into the first living cell."
New Scientist, 12th July 2003 p24-39

"Almost a century and a half [after Darwin] the origin of life remains one of the great unsolved problems of science."
"It is one thing for a primitive cell to be painstakingly designed and manufactured by a team of trained organic chemists in a laboratory full of expensive equipment, quite another for it to happen spontaneously in the rough and tumble of the natural world... The range and diversity of the theories serve to confirm that, to date, we really don't have much of a clue about how or where life began, or how long it took."
Paul Davies, New Scientist, 11th February 2006 p.48

And, by the way, organic chemists are nowhere near making a cell in their laboratories!

Although many scientists, both in the past and at present, are believers in a Deity, scientific theories cannot offer God as a source of the origin of anything. This is regarded as a god-of-the-gaps in our scientific knowledge. So theories have to assume that life on earth evolved by natural processes.

One such explaination is:

"Living complexity is indeed orders of magnitude too improbable to have come about by chance. But only if we assume that all the luck has come in one fell swoop. When cascades of small chance

steps accumulate, you can reach prodigious heights of adaptive complexity. The cumulative build-up is evolution, its guiding force is natural selection ... There has to be an ultimate source of new genetic variation, and it is mutation."
Professor Richard Dawkins, New Scientist, 17th September 2005 p. 31

Dawkins ignores the fact that his cascades of small chance steps cannot accumulate, since until a living cell could reproduce, natural selection would have nothing to work on. Moreover, this cascade of steps of syntheses of organic intermediates involves reversible reactions, with the equilibrium positions favouring the starting materials rather than the products. Even in a chemistry laboratory where useful intermediates could be isolated by skilled chemists, the yield from each step would be small. The total yield from a chain of steps would be infinitesimal, and without the intelligent chemists nothing would be achieved.

Space invaders?

It follows then that if life did evolve here, the chances are that it has evolved on other planets beyond our Solar System. The SETI programme, the search for extra-terrestrial intelligence, spends considerable resources scanning the heavens looking for radio signals that carry information from evolved civilisations of intelligent beings. Science fiction books, films and games are based on this notion. We are looking for a non-random signal from another world that carries information with meaning and purpose. Such a signal must then have come from an intelligent source. Yet when we look at the sequence of nucleotides in the grass under our feet we find there a non-random signal that carries information with meaning and purpose.

Take note that the source of genetic information, with all its complexity and interdependence, is an Intelligence of a very high order.

CHAPTER 3

Humans, apes and worms

The English naturalist Charles Darwin is said to have put the theory of organic evolution on a scientific basis with the publication of his book *On the Origin of Species* in 1859. Within a few short years the scientific community had accepted his ideas. Not wishing to be left behind (as the Church had been with the paradigm shift of Copernicus and Galileo) the clergy soon sought ways of reinterpreting the Scriptures to bring them up-to-date with modern science. The first chapter of Genesis was seen as a myth, not even written by Moses. The 'days' of Creation were clearly not intended to be taken as literal 24 hour periods. Some, wanting to retain the literal days, invented a Gap of many aeons between the first and second verses of the Bible in which the required millions of years of evolution could be accommodated.

Particularly in Germany the Higher Critics decided that the Bible should be analysed in the same fashion as any ancient text, on the assumption that it was not, as it claimed, inspired by God. Miracles were out. The Resurrection and Second Coming were 'spiritualized'. The six-day Creation and the worldwide Flood were seen as legends on a par with, and copied from, ancient Sumerian writings.

This two-pronged attack by science and theology left the authority of the Scriptures severely compromised. The basis of ethical standards had been undermined. Those who kept to the old paths were labelled religious fundamentalists and academia closed ranks to exclude them.

But in recent years there has been a partial reversal of these changes. Biblical fundamentalism is making a comeback in some parts of the church. These are the only churches to buck the trend of falling numbers in their congregations. Also, within the scientific community there are rumblings of dissent over evolution theory. Opinion polls tell us that the general population is no longer enamoured with Darwinism.

As reported in *BBC online*, 26th January 2006, the Horizon TV programme commissioned a MORI poll in which 2000 people were asked if Creation should be taught in schools. A total of 39% were in favour of creationism/Intelligent Design (ID) being taught, with 48% favouring evolution. Given more than one choice, 44% chose creationism, 41% ID and 69% evolution theory. This means that 31% of people in the UK do not want evolution taught in schools.

The Royal Society reacted to the MORI poll result by putting out a statement against teaching creationism/ID, and commissioned the atheist Professor Steve Jones to give a lecture entitled 'Why evolution theory is right and creationism is wrong'.

The Times Educational Supplement for 10th March 2006 announced that the OCR and Edexcel examination boards have produced new biology syllabuses where students are made aware of biblical creationism. So it seems that the controversy will be discussed in the classroom. Much must depend on individual teachers when explaining such emotive material.

Darwin's two mistakes

Evolution theory is now seen by many to be less soundly based on scientific principles than nineteenth century followers had supposed. Firstly, for all its claim to address the question of the origin of species, **Darwin's book merely dealt with variations within a kind of creature - finches' beaks, turtles' shells, breeds of dogs and pigeons.**

"Charles Darwin himself pointed out the observable changes wrought by pigeon fanciers and dog breeders. A century later biologists showed that peppered moths in England's industrial

heartland had evolved darker colours to camouflage themselves against soot-blackened trees. And by the end of the 20th century everyone knew that bacteria, insects and weeds were able to evolve resistance to antibiotics and pesticides within a few years."
New Scientist, 9th July 2005 p. 28

But was Darwin justified in extrapolating from this 'micro-evolution' to the macro-evolution of protozoa-to-people? He proposed that single-celled organisms evolved into multi-celled invertebrates that in turn developed into fish, then amphibians and so on up his tree of life to humans.

Secondly, Darwin spoke of natural selection as a mechanism for evolving ever greater biological complexity. Does natural selection have the ability to build new genetic information? Darwin wrote in the mid 19th century and it was another hundred years before the study of genetics and molecular biology developed detailed knowledge. It is now apparent that mutations lose rather than gain genetic information. Let us look at the basis of micro-evolution: In most cases the genomes of creatures contain more than one gene that can do a particular job. They are called alleles. Under certain circumstances, as with a change of climate, those members of a population having the allele that is best suited to the changed conditions will be at an advantage over the rest. They will be healthier and will pass on their fitter genes to future generations. Over time there will be a population shift. In the case of humans, darker skinned people are selected for sunnier climes. Shorter, stockier folk are best suited for cold climates such as Lapland. One allele is not necessarily dominant under a particular condition, so that even within members of one family the colour of hair and eyes can vary. As the 19th century priest-geneticist Gregor Mendel discovered, rather than breeding leading to an averaging out of characteristics, offspring will inherit traits from one or other parent. This kind of variation does not constitute macro-evolution. Even where the variants do not naturally interbreed, they are nevertheless still of the same kind.

Short-legged dog

Photo by Vij Sodera

Where dogs have been artificially bred to develop certain desirable characteristics, some alleles may be lost. The pure-bred dog will have less genetic information in its genome than a mongrel. It may be less healthy and require more attention from the vet, even though it may have butterfly ears or a pointer's nose. Artificial selection may proceed to the point where the pup's head is too large for natural birth, and caesarean operations are needed. Yet even between widely differing breeds, there is 99.85% similarity between the genomes. They are the same kind.

The point is that there are limits to the amount of variation tolerated by natural or artificial selection. Even with such comparatively simple organisms as bacteria, these limits are defined, as bacteriologist Professor Alan Linton has expressed. Alan Linton, Emeritus Professor of Bacteriology, University of Bristol, wrote a review of S J Gould's book *The Triumph of Evolution and the Failure of Creationism*:

> "But where is the experimental evidence? None exists in the literature claiming that one species has been shown to evolve into another. Bacteria, the simplest form of independent life, are ideal for this kind of study, with generation times of 20 to 30 minutes, and populations achieved in 18 hours. But throughout

150 years of the science of bacteriology, there is no evidence that one species of bacteria has changed into another, in spite of the fact that populations have been exposed to potent chemical and physical mutagens and that, uniquely, bacteria possess extra-chromosomal, transmissible plasmids."

The Times Higher Educational Supplement, 20th April 2001

Macro-evolution is not, then, an extension of micro-evolution.

Looking at natural selection, we have seen that it explains why dark skins are favoured for humans in sunny climes. It explains why air-borne seeds with small 'wings' are found on wind-swept islands, since large winged seeds get blown right out to sea and are lost. It explains why, when certain types of food are available, finches with particular beak shapes are favoured because finches that cannot cope with the food go hungry.

However, it is not possible for the environment to select genetic information that is not already present, so natural selection is not a creative process.

"The micro-evolutionary process that adequately describes evolution in a population is an utterly inadequate account of the earth's biota".

Review of Natural Selection by G C Williams OUP. Nature, 3rd June 1993 p. 408

Natural selection is capable of weeding out harmful mutations - survival of the fittest - but it cannot provide the genetic information to make the fit even fitter. So natural selection is a conserving process, not a creative mechanism. Darwin's idea that macro-evolution is simply micro-evolution writ large is incorrect, and his proposed mechanism of natural selection is inadequate for macro-evolution. Natural selection as an explanation of variation within a kind was however a big advance in our understanding as Edward Blyth (1835), Darwin and Wallace noted.

Fossils and evolution theory

Geologists have noted that the fossils in the world's sedimentary rocks are in fairly ordered layers, and that in general the simplest organisms are at the base of their 'geological column' with fish, land creatures, birds and man in progressively 'more recent' layers. This has been interpreted as a record of evolutionary history.

Darwin himself saw the fossil record as the weak point in his thesis, because no intermediate forms between the kinds had left fossils.

> "Geology assuredly does not reveal any such finely graduated organic chain; and this, perhaps, is the most obvious and serious objection which can be urged against the theory."
> Charles Darwin, Origin of Species

More than a century later, the links were still missing.

> "The extreme rarity of transitional forms in the fossil record persists as the trade secret of palaeontology. The evolutionary trees that adorn our textbooks have data only at the tips and nodes of the branches; the rest is inference, however reasonable, not the evidence of fossils."
> S.J. Gould, Natural History, 86 (5): p. 13 (1977)

Moreover, those creatures that had not become extinct had not evolved over time. The fossils and present day specimens showed only minor variations.

> "Frogs that would not look out of place in your garden were hopping around in Arizona 190 million years ago, according to two palaeontologists. They have found the oldest fossil of a frog yet discovered. The frog ... is helping to solve the mystery of how and where frogs and toads evolved the unique body plan that has kept them one leap ahead of the competition."
> New Scientist, 16th September 1995 p. 20

If the frogs have not evolved any further in the past alleged 190 my, one wonders how it will help to solve the mystery of how they evolved at all. Keeping one leap ahead of the competition gives the erroneous impression that it has continued to evolve - a leap of the imagination!

> "According to the fossil record, bats were soaring in the sky at least 55 million years ago. These ancient flyers, says evolutionary biologist Nancy Simmonds of New York City's American Museum of Natural History, were 'virtually indistinguishable from today's echo-locating bats'."
> Time (USA) 21st August 1995

Echo-locating apparatus is pretty advanced technology that we only began to catch up with at the time of the Second World War. Having evolved so far, why should these bats be content with sitting on their laurels for 55 my?

Fossil Bat

Examples of fossil stasis could be multiplied. The fossil record is no longer seen by the experts as supporting evolution theory, though the idea persists in school texts and in media discussions. So where is the evidence for a naturalistic origin of species?

Genetics and evolution theory

Towards the end of the 20th century the science of genetics was really getting into its stride. Faster, cheaper ways of studying the genetic make-up of creatures (their genomes or gene content, and their proteomes or protein content) held out the hope that this data would show an evolutionary progression from simple to complex creatures. It doesn't. There are no simple genomes. It has been noted that the DNA and proteins constitute coded information together with the means of translating that code into life-supporting systems and behaviour. Codes and their translation belong to the realms of intelligent design, according to Information Theory.

Humans, apes and worms

As well as genes, or exons, the chromosomes contain long sequences called introns, whose functions were not initially appreciated. In the 19th century, when evolutionists found organs in our bodies whose uses were not known, they labelled them 'vestigial', remnants from our evolutionary past, no longer required. However, over time, uses have been found for most so-called vestigial organs. At the close of the 20th century, evolutionists labelled the introns between the genes as 'junk DNA'. After all, if organisms have evolved all the way from single cells since 3.8 billion years ago, there must be remnants of DNA still around from previous forms. The evolutionists are now beginning to have second thoughts. Could this junk be part of a complex design?

> "The exons in the genes form the information bits of code and the introns ['junk' DNA] are the error correcting bits."
> New Scientist, 26th June 1993 p. 15

> "The human genome contains the largest proportion of junk DNA of any species. Could it be our junk DNA, rather than our genes, that makes us who we are?"
> New Scientist, 19th November 2005 p. 54

An engineer is likely to use the same mechanism to do a comparable job in more than one structure. After all, there is no point in re-inventing the wheel. Even so, we find very similar genes in widely differing organisms. One would not expect the genomes of tiny worms and man to bear much comparison. But they do.

> "Nearly 75% of human genes have some counterpart in nematodes - millimetre long soil-dwelling worms - but that does not mean that a worm is three-quarters of the way to becoming a person."
> New Scientist, 15th May 1999 p. 26

And what of mice and men?

> "Celera, the company based in Rockville, Maryland, which has

compared the mouse chromosome 16 with human DNA found
that of the 731 mouse genes, only 14 lacked a counterpart in
humans."
New Scientist, 8th June 2002 p. 23

It has been argued that where evolution comes up with a useful idea,
it hangs on to it over millions of years of change, so that genes that
functioned well in mice are retained through to the evolution of
humans. The difficulty with this notion is that the coded information is
millions of units long, carefully folded with accompanying proteins so
that all parts are accessible for decoding with RNA. Chance and time
cannot turn up anything like this. The mutations of alleged evolution
would corrupt genetic information.

"Chromosomes actually contain about twice as much protein as
DNA, and it now seems that these proteins have their own code
that controls the activity of the DNA wound around them…No
longer written off as mere packaging, the proteins that help
parcel DNA into chromosomes play a part in controlling which
genes are expressed."
New Scientist, 15th March 2003 p. 35

Chance changes would also produce lots of useless material. Design
would produce just the right quantity of custom-made parts.

How have man's [30,000] genes been orchestrated to produce 250
different cell types that become assembled to form a human body?
Chance would give an almost infinite number of cell types.
New Scientist, 5th June 1993 p. 46 review of Origin of Order by S A
Kaufman, OUP

Even small changes can lead to catastrophic results and so the neo-
Darwinian recipe of mutation regulated by natural selection would
appear to be a non-starter.

"Our DNA contains more than 80,000 genes [since revised to 30,000 or less] that control all the workings of our bodies. Yet amid this complexity, even the tiniest of errors can be devastating: Fatal diseases such as sickle-cell anaemia and cystic fibrosis are caused by simple, inherited genetic defects. Similarly, damage to DNA can trigger the kind of uncontrolled cell growth that leads to cancer."
New Scientist, 7th February 1998 p. 36

A good design that is subject to mutations requires an error detecting system along with a means of fixing the problems during replication of cells. Chance mutations will certainly not turn up a brilliant quality control plus repair mechanism.

"Enzymes that repair DNA may check for mutations by sending electrons along sections of the strand, in much the same way that electricians test for faults in circuits. The mechanism might explain how enzymes locate problems in the genome fast enough to correct them."
New Scientist, 18th October 2003 p. 10

Could natural selection help here? No chance! While the organism was waiting the many generation times needed to gradually hone the mechanism to perfection (assuming that it could) the absence of a control and repair mechanism would result in extinction.

Three claimed evolutionary jumps:

1. Invertebrates to Vertebrates

For evolution to be true, creatures without backbones, the invertebrates such as snails, must have somehow evolved into vertebrates such as fish. Can something survive while its exo-skeleton, such as a shell, somehow becomes a set of bones or cartilage supporting the flesh?

Has Darwin had his day?

"In On the Origin of Species, Darwin proposed that new species were the result of the slow accumulation of small random variations, with the environment dictating which variations survived. But there is little evidence in the fossil record for the transitional forms predicted by this 'gradualist' mechanism, such as those between invertebrates and vertebrates. Natural selection undoubtedly fine-tunes the adaptation of a species to the environment, but one finds little evidence that it can give rise to major biological novelties."
New Scientist, 13th February 1999 p. 12

Fish, supposedly the earliest vertebrates, are somewhere at the bottom of the evolutionist's tree of life. Because of their imagined place in the evolutionary hierarchy they have been thought unintelligent. But recent research has sprung a surprise. Fish have been shown to have a good memory and are smarter than many dumb animals on higher branches of their 'tree'. Small wonder that folk sit on a river bank all day and catch nothing more than colds!

"Fish are more intelligent than they appear. In many areas, such as memory, their cognitive powers match or exceed those of 'higher' vertebrates, including non-human primates...The widespread notion of fish as stupid is partially grounded in a traditional reading of evolution. According to this, fish are the most primitive vertebrates and evolution has progressed by gradual linear gradients, from fish through amphibians, reptiles, birds, mammals and primates to humans. The 'higher' the species, the more complex its brain structure, intelligence and behaviour."
New Scientist, 12th June 2004 p. 41

2. Dinosaurs to Birds

Another proposed evolutionary change that has hit the headlines in recent years is that of dinosaurs becoming birds. Darwin's bulldog, T. H. Huxley, had made this claim in the 19th century, and with the opening up to the West of rich fossil deposits in Liaoning Province in China at the end of the 20th century, expectations apparently began to be realized. This writer was a guest at the London Natural History Museum's preview of their display of a claimed feathered dinosaur. Although there were lots of real flight feathers hanging around to set the scene, when one looked through the microscope at the fossil one saw only fibres but no feathers. It was a triumph of wishful thinking over observation that surely fooled only the dedicated believer.

At the turn of the century National Geographic Magazine, which normally prides itself on checking the evidence thoroughly, published an article with convincing photographs of a feathered dinosaur called Archaeoraptor. It had been dug up in China and appeared to be a bird with feathers but with a reptilian tail. Unfortunately for the reputation of National Geographic, that is precisely what it was. Some inscrutable Chinaman had glued together the front of a fossil bird and the tail of a reptile. When you want something badly enough it is possible to overlook the flaws and even pay good money for a fake.

> "The idea of feathered dinosaurs and the theropod origin of birds is being actively promulgated by a cadre of zealous scientists acting in concert with certain editors at Nature and National Geographic who themselves have become outspoken and highly biased proselytisers of the faith. Truth and careful scientific weighing of evidence have been among the first casualties in their program, which is now fast becoming one of the grander scientific hoaxes of our age - the palaeontological equivalent of cold fusion."
>
> An open letter, 1st November 1999, from Storrs L. Olson, Curator of birds, National Museum of Natural History, Smithsonian Institute, Washington DC to National Geographic Society Committee for Research and Exploration after they claimed that: 'Archaeoraptor liaoningensis was a dino-bird intermediate form. The fossil was a fake; a dinosaur tail glued to a fossil bird'.

This letter, also reported in *New Scientist*, 29th January 2000 p. 12, added:

Has Darwin had his day?

> "There is not one undisputed example of a dinosaur with feathers. None. The public deserves to know this."

Apart from the need to change from a cold-blooded to a warm-blooded metabolism, and from a two-way lung system of the reptile to a one-way air flow of the bird, there is the question of the digits used by each from their pentadactyl limbs.

> "All vertebrate limbs start in embryonic life with five potential fingers, but some develop more than others to form the mature hand. It has recently been shown that birds have three bony fingers formed from digits II, III and IV. Gilbert Chin comments: 'These findings have implications for the evolutionary relationship between birds and theropod dinosaurs which display a I, II, III digit identity.'"
> Science, vol. 297, p. 1611, 16th September 2002

> "Biologists in the US ... say that a comparison of dinosaur claws with bird wings and feet contradicts the widespread theory that birds evolved from small, flesh-eating dinosaurs 150 million years ago ... birds and theropods are missing different digits ...'As a result, it's almost inconceivable that one group derived from the other' Feduccia says ... birds have retained the middle three digits during evolution. The outer two, numbers one and five, have almost entirely disappeared. But ... in theropods, the fourth and fifth digits are greatly diminished or have disappeared altogether. Feduccia maintains that animals which had lost these digits could not then evolve into birds that lacked one and five ... Other experts agree. They are doing a first-class job of ... making us re-examine the evidence."
> New Scientist, 1st November 1997 p. 20

The world's most valuable fossil is the London specimen of Archaeopteryx. This bird has flight feathers, but also features found in some reptiles. The tail has fused bones and the wings have hooks on them. The beak has teeth. (Some birds today have hooks on their wings, and some extinct birds had teeth. Some reptiles have teeth while others haven't.) The London NHM archaeopteryx is the only one whose skull is not crushed flat by burial. Recently the skull was subjected to CT scans, and was found to be completely avian. The brain showed none of the expected half-way qualities of a missing link.

> "What these [CT] scans revealed was that, beneath the skull, archaeopteryx had much in common with a modern bird... 'It definitely had a flight-ready brain.' One revelation was the size and shape of the delicate semi-circular canals in the inner ear, which are crucial for balance. They were highly arced like those of modern birds, a trait associated with an acrobatic or aerobatic lifestyle. As for the brain itself, archaeopteryx had massive bird-like visual centres jutting out from either side of the brain, and the apparatus for a superb sense of hearing. But perhaps the most notable feature was a hefty cerebellum - the brain's 'autopilot', where sensory information is coordinated and integrated. Its relative size was far larger than even the birdiest dinosaurs, which include velociraptor. That is the real neural advance, says Rowe. 'Integration is ultimately what it is all about - how you put senses together and make decisions.'
> New Scientist, 21st May 2005 p. 34

3. Apes to Humans

Scans also play a part in the third of our examples of a proposed evolutionary jump, that from ape to man. Man is upright, at least in his mode of walking. His bipedalism requires a more precise balancing mechanism than creatures that go on all fours. Fossil men and apes can be distinguished by examining the labyrinth, a hard bony structure of the inner ear that is preserved during fossilisation.

Professor Bernard Wood of University of Liverpool did computerised tomography scans of inner ears of fossil apes and man. Man, who is bipedal, has a more complex pattern of the labyrinth than knuckle-walking apes. Man requires a more sophisticated balancing mechanism.

Archaeopteryx fossil

Humans, apes and worms

Homo erectus fossils have human patterns while Australopithecines have an ape-like pattern of labyrinth. There are no intermediate patterns.

> "Among the fossil hominids, the earliest to demonstrate the modern human morphology is Homo Erectus. In contrast, the semi-circular dimension in crania from Southern Africa attributed to Australopithecus and Paranthropus resemble those of the extinct great apes."
> Nature, 23rd June 1994 p. 645

Scans of the ear structures of modern humans, the so-called hominin *H. heidelbergensis* and chimpanzees show similarities in the abilities to appreciate speech with the first two, but not apes.

> "Spanish and American researchers used CT scans to measure the bones and spaces in the outer and middle ears of five specimens, thought to be *Homo heidelbergensis*. They then worked out how well the hearing apparatus they found could respond to various frequencies. Like modern humans, the hominids' ears would have been sensitive to frequencies in the range from 2 to 4 kilohertz, suggesting that they, too, could distinguish the sounds of speech. Chimpanzees' ears are relatively insensitive at those frequencies."
> New Scientist, 26th June 2004 p. 16

Not only are chimps not in the same league as men and women when it comes to conversation, but their sense of musical harmony leaves much to be desired.

> "Monkeys do not prefer sounds that are harmonious to human ears, suggesting that people have a unique appreciation of music...Even young infants enjoy hearing consonant intervals more, suggesting that people are hard-wired with the preference at birth.
> New Scientist, 25th September 2004 p. 17

Chimp and human DNA

Now that the genomes of man and chimpanzee have been completed, we find that they have a great deal of information in common. Chimps and man have very similar body plans and perform many similar bodily functions such as respiration, digestion and reproduction. So similarities are inevitable. One cannot decide merely from the data whether these are the result of an evolutionary relationship or of having the same Designer.

While the study of just the genes of the two kinds, chimps and man, shows a 98.5 per cent correspondence, the whole genomes have only a 95 per cent similarity.

> "We're told that we share 98.5 per cent of our DNA with chimps, a figure touted so widely it has almost become a mantra. Now it seems that number is wrong. We actually share less than 95 per cent of our genetic material, so the difference is three times as great as was thought."
> New Scientist, 28th September 2002 p. 20

> "Contrary to what you might think, large differences in DNA, not small ones, separate apes and monkeys from both humans and each other. Scientists believed that differences between primates were mainly the result of variations in individual DNA letters. But a detailed comparison of human chromosome 21 with corresponding regions of genetic material in chimpanzees, orang-utans, rhesus macaques and woolly monkeys show the differences affect great chunks of DNA.
> 'There are large deletions and insertions sprinkled throughout the chromosome,' says Kelly Frazer of Perlegen Sciences Co. of California, USA."
> New Scientist, 15th March 2003 p. 26 Genome Research, vol. 13 p. 341

This is seen as an unbridgeable gap for evolution.

Humans, apes and worms

Chimpanzees

Dr. Patrick Gill, FRCR writes: "As there are at least 3,000 million units in the DNA chain, the real mismatch between humans and chimpanzees works out at 30 million per cell, which any scientist or doctor knows to be an unbridgeable chasm."
Medical Journal of Australia, vol. 152, April 1990

In addition, all these differences have a massive effect on the proteins produced by the two genomes.

"A comparison of the chimpanzee's chromosome 22 and its counterpart, human chromosome 21, shows that just 1.44 per cent of the chromosomes' 33.3 million DNA bases are different. The study also revealed nearly 68,000 insertions or deletions of DNA, most of which were only a few bases long. But because each gene contains hundreds of thousands of bases, even these differences are enough to alter more than 80 per cent of the proteins produced by those genes, according to the International Chimpanzee Chromosome 22 Consortium."
New Scientist, 29th May 2004 p. 16

Recent common ancestor

Palaeontologists offer dates of a few million years for their fossil humans. However, a study of genes of people of various ethnic groups leads us to conclude that the common ancestor of today's families lived only thousands of years ago. There was evidently a population bottleneck just a few thousand years ago. The histories of most ethnic groups speak of a world-wide flood in which eight persons survived. When we come to look at sedimentation rates in the next chapter, this idea will not seem impossible.

> "In recording it [disappearing Amazonian languages] you are also getting down the stories and folklore. If these are lost a huge part of a people's history goes. These stories often have a common root that speaks of a real event, not just a myth. For example, every Amazonian society ever studied has a legend about a great flood."
> New Scientist, 31st January 2004 p. 44

Studies have been made of the mutational differences in the mitochondrial DNA of women of various ethnic groups today, and in the DNA on the Y chromosomes of men. Estimates of mutation rates enabled the geneticists to come up with embarrassingly recent dates for the common human ancestor, not millions of years. Then more accurate values for mutation rates were published in Nature Genetics, giving dates of just a few thousand years.

> Mutational differences between the mitochondrial DNA of women of various ethnic groups leads to the conclusion that we are all descended from one woman, Mitochondrial Eve, estimated from mutation rates to have lived 100,000 to 200,000 years ago.
> Nature, 1st January 1987 p. 31

> And Mutational differences between the DNA on the Y chromosomes of men of various ethnic groups leads to

the conclusion that we are all descended from one man, Y chromosome Adam, estimated to have lived up to 200,000 years ago.

Nature, 23rd November 1995

But Parsons et al: A team of geneticists found the rate of mutation of mtDNA is twenty times higher than expected. This dates Y chromosome Adam and mitochondria Eve between 5,000 and 10,000 years ago.

Nature Genetics, vol. 15 no. 4, 1997 p. 363-7

"…an individual that is the genealogical ancestor of all living humans existed just a few thousand years ago. Had you entered any village on earth in around 3000BC, the first person you would have met would probably have been your ancestor!"

Nature, vol. 431 p. 562 (2004)

Incidentally, although we talk of various ethnic groups, it must be remembered that we are all variations of a kind.

"It was European naturalists in Victorian times who popularised the notion of race. But trouble set in as soon as the concept was subjected to systematic study, and all attempts to unambiguously assign individuals to one race or another according to their physical characteristics have failed. Attempts to use genetics initially fared no better. Looking at single genes, researchers found more variety within racial groups than between them."

New Scientist, 11th June 2005 p. 3

Some doubted

Having looked at some difficulties with the evolutionary view of the origin of species in this chapter, see what some prominent scientists think of the subject.

Has Darwin had his day?

John Chaikowski writes:

"Evolutionists have 'Physics Envy'. They tell the public that the science behind evolution is the same science that sent people to the moon and cures diseases. It's not.

"The science behind evolution is not empirical, but forensic. Because evolution took place in history, its scientific investigations are after the fact - no testing, no observations, no repeatability, no falsification, nothing at all like Physics... I think this is what the public discerns - that evolution is just a bunch of just-so stories disguised as legitimate science."
Geotimes, vol. 50, April 2005, p.165

Common ancestory of
different ethnic groups

CHAPTER 4

What can the rocks tell us?

Were you to ask most evolutionists what offers the best evidence for their belief, they would point you to the fossil record. The sedimentary rocks are in layers that often extend over whole continents. They contain fossils of petrified plants and animals, many of which can be recognised from today's flora and fauna, while others are of organisms that have become extinct. The lower layers, which must be the oldest sediments (even if only by moments), contain fossils of comparatively simple life forms that are considered as primitive. The more 'recent' layers at the top of the 'geological column' contain fossils of creatures said to be more highly evolved. The layers are believed to have been laid down slowly and gradually, since sea floor sediments today take a long time to accumulate. This interpretation was formulated in the 18th and 19th centuries by men like Smith (who surveyed Britain in order to build its canal system), Hutton and Lyell. Charles Lyell's book *Principles of Geology* was read by Darwin during his HMS Beagle cruise, and influenced his view that the earth must be many millions of years old. Darwin proposed a 'tree of life' where single-celled protozoa were the 'roots' and invertebrates such as snails developed into fish that then crawled out onto the land as amphibians and reptiles. These then evolved into mammals and birds. Finally primates evolved into humans. The whole story of life on earth was apparently written in stone for all to read.

The millions of years seemingly needed for bacteria to evolve into bananas and bonobo chimps were also required for the miles of thickness of sedimentary rocks (limestone, sandstone, mudstone, chalk, etc.) slowly deposited and eroded. The biblical notion of heavens and earth created in six days only some six thousand years ago was now challenged by the new science of Geology. And if the first chapter of the Bible was so wide of the truth, what credence could be given to the rest of it. Noah floating above a world-wide flood with all the animal kinds, God coming as a man, doing miracles, rising from the dead and coming at some future time could be safely discounted. Churchmen salvaged what they could by saying that Creation was a story that was not intended by its writers to be taken literally. Days represented long periods of time, or there was a gap of unspecified duration between the first two verses of the first chapter of Genesis. It would seem that science showed that God used the evolutionary process to create everything, leaving little trace of His handiwork. In which case, was there really a Creator? It was now intellectually respectable, if not mandatory, to be an atheist.

The new catastrophism

The close of the 20th century saw a challenge to this 18th century view of slow and gradual sedimentation processes. Derek Ager, Geology professor at Swansea in South Wales, had pointed out that where a sedimentary layer contained boulders in a fine matrix of sand or clay, it must have been deposited in a fast moving slurry. The laying down of such turbidite layers had even been witnessed when an earthquake on the Grand Banks at Newfoundland had caused a slippage of the continental shelf around Canada's Atlantic coast. It happened on the 18th November 1929 and the precise timing and velocity of the sediment layer's movement were recorded by the severing, one after the other, of thirteen trans-Atlantic cables as the flow spread over the ocean floor. The flow travelled at 50 mph and covered 500 miles in 13 hours. The resultant layer was two to three feet thick and covered an area of over 100,000 square miles. It had the same texture as other turbidity layers in the geological column. Ager had realized that conglomerates, cross-bedded sandstone, breccias and turbidites had been deposited by storms and catastrophes in hours rather than millions of years.

Sharply folded sedimentary layers show that mountain building earth movements have been rapid. Great thicknesses of what must have been freshly deposited wet and plastic layers have been twisted without shattering.

Rapid carving out of landscapes has been witnessed since 1963 on the newly formed volcanic island of Surtsey, off the coast of Iceland.

> Despite the somewhat haphazard arrival of species, we now have a fully functioning ecosystem... The plants support insects that attract birds that bring more plants... The island [Surtsey, a volcano formed in 1963] has excited geographers, who marvel that canyons, gullies and other land features that typically take tens of thousands or millions of years to form were created in less than a decade."
> New Scientist, 28th January 2006 p. 48

On May 18th 1980, Mount St. Helens, a volcano in Washington State, USA, exploded violently, depositing tens of feet of finely layered material in that day. Each fine layer had not taken a year or a season, but just a moment to settle.

The fresh deposits from the eruption blocked the course of a river so that a head of water built up. Subsequently a mudslide burst through the freshly laid sediments, carving out a canyon one tenth the scale of Arizona's Grand Canyon. This latter is said to have been worn down by the Colorado River over millions of years, but comparison with the canyon at Mt. St. Helens argues that the Grand Canyon was similarly formed catastrophically, by a mudslide while still wet.

Experiments in laboratory flumes at Marseilles and Colorado Universities using slurries of mixed fine and coarse sand in water have shown that layers are indeed deposited rapidly. These results were published by Guy Berthault and co-workers by France's National Academy.

What can the rocks tell us?

> "The stratification of poured granular mixtures into layers according to particle size has long been identified as an important mechanism by which such materials segregate."
> Nature, 8th January 1998 p. 136

Chalk beds stretching around the world are composed of myriads of tiny shells, being virtually 100 per cent pure calcium carbonate. During alleged millions of years of deposition in water, surely impurities would sully the pristine whiteness of the chalk. One possible explanation is that carbon dioxide released by large-scale volcanism caused a blooming of these shell fish, and that rapidly moving water swept them together into thick beds. Such world-wide chalk beds suggest a world-wide flood, and history tells of such an event. All people groups have such a folk memory, with details coinciding with much of the Genesis flood story.

So does the process of fossilization take a very long time? Apparently not. Wood has been opalised by immersion in a spring rich in silica mineral in less than a decade. Fossils have been made artificially in only weeks using bacteria.

> "In laboratory experiments palaeontologists have shown how bacteria can turn flesh into stone. In only a few weeks, they managed to mimic a mineralization process that takes millions of years in nature."
> New Scientist, 19th March 1994 p. 17

Oil and coal have been produced rapidly in the laboratory also. It takes high temperatures and pressures, but not millions of years.

> "We can simulate natural oil generation in the laboratory from organic-rich source rock."
> New Scientist, 17th August 2002 p. 17

Fossil evidence also points to rapid burial. Upright fossil trees are found in many parts of the world. A good example can be seen in the grounds

Fossil Crynoid

Living crynoid

Photo by Andrew Dickinson

What can the rocks tell us?

of London's Natural History Museum. If the sediments that buried it had been laid down over thousands of years, the top of the tree would have rotted away before it was fully covered. The lack of roots suggests that such trees were snapped off and transported before being buried in slurry in which they were petrified. Crynoids, small marine animals also known as sea lilies (see illustration), die and decompose leaving a scattering of ossicles. However, fossil crinoids are petrified whole. They were buried alive before they could decompose. Clams and other bivalves have a muscle that holds the shells tightly closed. At death the muscle relaxes and the two shells open out like a butterfly's wings. In the fossil record bivalves are found tightly closed. Again this indicates that they were buried alive, by rapid inundation.

The fossil record is characterized by fossil graveyards, where millions of creatures, such as fish, are found buried together. This speaks of catastrophe. Similarly, mixed beds of land and marine fossils speak of the sea inundating the land. A natural disaster such as the alleged tsunami resulting from a crater off the Yucatan coast in the geological past produced just such a mixed bed of jumbled fossils.

> "The deposits include oysters from bays, snails from marshes and foraminifera that float in open water, along with impact debris such as solidified molten rock, says Lawton. As the tsunami retreated it dumped these together...The team argues that the tsunami could also have messed up fossil records elsewhere."
> New Scientist, 12th February 2005 p. 15

It seems more than likely that igneous rocks are also deposited quickly. A layer of basalt known as the Deccan Traps covers much of Western India. The flow is a mile thick and extends almost 200,000 square miles. Volcanism on such a scale is unheard of in historic times and must have occurred at a time when the earth's crust was undergoing violent changes.

Has Darwin had his day?

"... colleagues from France, India and the UK have shown that volcanic eruptions formed the Deccan Traps more quickly than previously thought."
New Scientist, 20th August 2005 p. 11

It has been said that long periods of time are needed for very large crystals to form in granite. Apparently this is not the case:

"Experimental data on crystallization rates suggest that many of the large crystals observed in granitic rocks could have grown in a matter of hours - certainly in no more than a few tens of years. Geological processes are commonly thought of as slow and continuous, but many are rapid and episodic. Granitic plutonism is of the latter kind."
J. D. Clemens, Proceedings of the Geologists' Association, vol. 116, pp. 9-16, 2005

So the nature of the stratagraphic record would appear to be very different from Lyell's view of millions of years of deposition. Ager suggested that the millions of years required for macro-evolution were quietly played out in the time periods between these catastrophic events, leaving no evidence of their passing. But could it be that macro-evolution hasn't happened and that the earth is not millions, let alone billions, of years old?

Written records only go back about 5,000 years. Agriculture and cities similarly date back only thousands of years, even when the dating involves big assumptions. Living trees go back to about the same time.

"No ring counts performed on any of the many stems of this 'tree' exceeded 2,100 years. The 11,000-year claim is based on extremely circumstantial evidence: a pollen record in a peat bog nearby...The oldest individual tree in the world is still a c.5,000 year-old specimen of bristle cone pine in Nevada."
Aljos Farjon, Royal Botanic Gardens Kew, in The Garden, September 1998

and

> " 'This tree was a seedling at the time of the building of the Great Pyramid and of Stonehenge' - Horticulturist Jared Milarch, who hopes to clone the world's oldest living tree, a 4,768-year-old bristle cone pine."
> New Scientist, 21st June 2003 p. 6

Of course, scientific dating methods, unlike historical dates, do go back for unimaginable periods of time. However the methods that give these dates contain assumptions which can sometimes be shown to give the wrong result. In a case brought to our notice by sedimentologist Dr. Guy Berthault in 2002, the different minerals in a sample of dacite gave widely varying dates. This is because not all the crystals melted in the 1986 eruption at Mt. St. Helens (not the 1980 one) so results varied from crystal to crystal. All the argon gas had not escaped when the K-Ar (potassium-argon) clock was reset in the molten magma. A long age by this method results from the large amount of argon-40 present. The period of time of the half life for the nuclear disintegration of K into both Ar and Ca involves further assumptions and uncertainties.

> The minerals in a sample of dacite, erupted from Mt St Helens in 1986, were dated by the potassium argon method as follows: pyroxene 2,800,000 years, amphibole 900,000 years and feldspar 340,000 years. Erupted magma contains solid crystals as well as liquid rock and gas, and the crystals retain argon.
> Guy Berthault, Sedimentologist, personal communication, 2002

Missing Links

What might one expect to find in the fossil record if it is a reflection of an evolutionary past? For one thing, as discussed above, we would expect a slow rate of sedimentation. On the Isle of Wight off the south coast of England, for instance, if you divide the depth of sediment by the postulated millions of years during which evolutionists claim the sediments were laid down, you get an average figure of one hair's breadth per year of deposition. Hardly sufficient to cover and fossilise anything! Also with this scenario, we might expect the creatures to have lived, died, been buried and petrified all at the same location. The evidence shows that fossils have been washed together under violent conditions. There was no Jurassic Era; all of the dinosaurs were washed and sorted by size, density and habitat into the beds we designate Jurassic.

If invertebrates with exo-skeletons gradually changed into fish with backbones, it is reasonable to suppose that there were a considerable number of partly changed intermediates, some of which should have left traces in the fossil record. There should be fossilised links between fish and amphibians, between reptiles and birds, and so on. There are no intermediates. The problem of the missing links was acknowledged by Charles Darwin in his *On the Origin of Species* in 1859.

> "Geology assuredly does not reveal any such finely graduated organic chain; and this, perhaps, is the most obvious and serious objection which can be urged against the theory."
> Charles Darwin, Origin of Species

Darwin fully expected that as the fossil record was further explored, many of the missing links would be found. Today the world's collections contain many millions of fossils, some just like today's creatures, some now extinct. But there are no examples of intermediate forms. This has been admitted by Stephen Jay Gould, who during his lifetime was perhaps America's most famous palaeontologist (fossil expert). He was so concerned with this weakness of evolution theory that Darwin had himself highlighted that, together with Niles Eldridge, he proposed that evolution was not gradual but sudden, leaving no intermediate forms. They called their new evolution theory Punctuated Equilibrium. They claimed that long periods of stasis during which no evolutionary changes occurred were punctuated by rapid and significant developments. Since these would have required a large number of big genetic mutations, critics argued that creatures could not survive such extreme change and be viable. However, Gould's honesty did bring the lack of transitional forms in the fossil record to the public's attention.

> "Gradualism was never proved from the rocks by Lyell and Darwin, but was rather imposed as a bias upon nature. …has had a profoundly negative impact by stifling hypotheses and by closing the minds of a profession towards reasonable empirical alternatives to the dogma of gradualism. Lyell won with rhetoric what he could not carry with data."
>
> S J Gould, Toward the vindication of punctuated change, in Berggren & Van Couvering (eds), Catastrophes and earth History: the new uniformitarianism, Princeton Univ. Press, 1984, pp. 14-16

[As an interesting aside, the BBC tried to set up a debate between Stephen Jay Gould and this author during Gould's last visit to the UK, and shortly before his death. As is the case with all high profile evolutionists, he refused the opportunity to cross swords with a creationist. To do so would, they say, lend credence to creationism. In fact, they cannot answer our arguments.]

Imaginative palaeontologists have 'discovered' missing Links from time to time, such as the inch long section of jaw bone found near Elgin in Scotland a few decades ago, and claimed to be part of the first land animal to crawl out of the sea! But where more data is amassed, the missing link finds have to be discarded. In April 2006, another 'intermediate' between fish and amphibians was reported. Named *Tiktaalik roseae*, it was fish-like but it could bend its neck to snatch animals from the land. Shortly afterwards, it was noted that it strongly resembled the African eel catfish *Channallabus apus*, a living fish that can also bend its neck.

> "The record of evolution is still surprisingly jerky and, ironically, we have even fewer examples of evolutionary transition than we had in Darwin's time. By this I mean that some of the classic cases of Darwinian change in the fossil record, such as the evolution of the horse in North America, have had to be

discarded or modified as a result of more detailed information - what appeared to be a nice simple progression when relatively few data were available now appears to be much more complex and much less gradualistic."
Dr. David Raup, Curator of Geology in Chicago Field Museum of Natural History Bulletin, vol. 50, no. 1, January 1979, p. 25

We have noted that the fossil Archaeopteryx, long claimed as the best example of an intermediate form, has a fully avian brain and flight feathers. The digits of dinosaurs and birds come from different parts of the pentdactyl limbs. The ear labyrinths of humans and apes are distinct. The missing links, despite Piltdown Man (1912 to 1953 R.I.P.) and Archaeoraptor, are still missing.

"Archaeoraptor is just the tip of the iceberg. There are scores of fake fossils out there, and they have cast a dark shadow over the whole field. When you go to these fossil shows, it's difficult to tell which ones are fake and which ones are not. I have heard there is a fake fossil factory in northeast China, in Liaoning Province, near the deposits where many of these recent alleged feathered dinosaurs were found."
Alan Feduccia, fossil bird expert. Discover, February 2003, p. 59

Stasis

Not only are there no intermediate forms between different kinds of creatures, but those types that have not become extinct are recognisably unchanged. This applies across the whole spectrum of creatures - fungi, sponges, insects, bats, and so on, as the following selection of quotes shows:

"Most plants have root fungi known as mycorrhizae that help them obtain nutrients such as phosphorus from the soil ... examined rocks from 460-million-year-old strata. They found fossilised structures closely resembling modern mycorrhizae."
New Scientist, 23rd September 2000 p. 21

What can the rocks tell us?

Silica spicules that stiffen sponges have been found in chert rock said to be 544 my old late Ediacarian (pre-Cambrian). "The spicules have the same shapes as those in modern sponges."
New Scientist, 12th April 1997 p. 19

"Dominican amber has preserved 20-million-year-old termites so exquisitely that even the microbes inside their guts are recognisable…The bugs look just like those found inside the termites' closest living relative, *M. Darwiniensis*, says Dolan."
New Scientist, 16th February 2002 p. 23

"A tiny harvestman [opinoid spider] is also present [among fossils at Bathgate, Scotland] the oldest known by 27 my and is apparently indistinguishable from modern forms."
New Scientist, 12th February 1994 p. 21

"The world's oldest known spider silk has been found preserved in a piece of amber 130 my old. While fossils reveal that spiders were equipped with silk-spinning glands as far back as 410 my ago, this is the oldest silk. The single 4 mm strand resembles silk from the complex aerial webs of modern orb-weaver or comb-footed spiders. The strand has tiny droplets spaced out along it that resemble those found on threads extending from the centre of aerial webs."
New Scientist, 9th August 2003 p. 24

"Bats have been an evolutionary enigma. That's because the oldest fossil bats look remarkably like modern ones, each having wings formed from membranes stretched between long fingers and ear structures designed for echolocation. No fossils of an animal intermediate between bats and their non-flying mammal ancestors have been found."
New Scientist, 13th November 2004 p. 16

The DNA that carries the genetic information of creatures is copied whenever a cell divides. Mistakes are monitored and repaired by a complex system that shouts design. Not only does the DNA degrade in the living creature, but after death it continues to be corrupted without recourse to repairs. Yet the journal *Nature* reported (10th June 1993 p536) that the DNA of a "120-135my old weevil in Lebanese amber" had been sequenced. Could DNA of such an unimaginable age survive and be read? We think not.

Climate changes

The Bible speaks of waters above the atmosphere before the worldwide flood. The thermosphere above our present atmosphere would have been capable of holding a great deal of water as superheated steam. Such a water vapour canopy would have been transparent to sunlight but would have blocked much harmful radiation such as that responsible for forming radio-carbon from atmospheric nitrogen. The increased barometric pressure would have slowed down heartbeat rates, which might explain the long life spans recorded in Genesis 5 and 11. (Today some patients have been successfully treated in containers under a high pressure, oxygen-rich atmosphere. Bleeding stops and healing of wounds is accelerated.) Perhaps this canopy of super-heated steam was precipitated at the time of the flood? As mentioned earlier, there is a great deal of extra-biblical evidence for a major flood from people groups around the world. The loss of this canopy would enable the earth to radiate heat back into space more readily. Warm post-flood seas would lead to high rates of evaporation. The clouds would condense to precipitate snow and ice at the polar regions where the Sun's rays gave less heat. This would lead to the ice age as ice flowed under its own weight, and spread out towards lower latitudes. Subsequently the melting ice would cause the sea levels to rise and land bridges to disappear as continents and islands became separated by the rising water.

While creatures are recognisably the same in the fossil record as their living descendants today, the fossil forms, particularly of plants and insects, are often considerably larger. Fossil ferns can be the size of today's tall trees, and dragonflies' wingspans as long as your arm.

What can the rocks tell us?

Insects breathe through their skin and a higher oxygen content in the atmosphere would allow them to grow large. Air bubbles trapped in Baltic amber have 35 per cent oxygen. Laboratory experiments using strips of dry paper showed that such a high concentration of oxygen would have been a fire risk. Yet more recent tests with green vegetation indicated that such an atmospheric composition would, after all, have been viable (at least for non-smokers).

"Our atmosphere could once have had a much higher proportion of oxygen - as much as 35 per cent - according to recent experiments…This fits the fossil evidence of the late Palaeozoic, around 240 million years ago. The giant insects of the era are thought to have needed a lot of oxygen to breathe. Also the existence of plants with thick, fire-resistant bark implies that oxygen levels were high enough to make fires more common, though not to destroy all forests."
New Scientist, 1st May 2004 p. 18

Many of the larger animals, such as dinosaurs and mammoths, have become extinct over the past few thousand years. (Yes, stories of living dinosaurs, as well as engravings and pictures, have persisted well into the Christian era. Lots of these have been collected in Dr. Bill Cooper's book *After the Flood*, available from CSM See page 118).

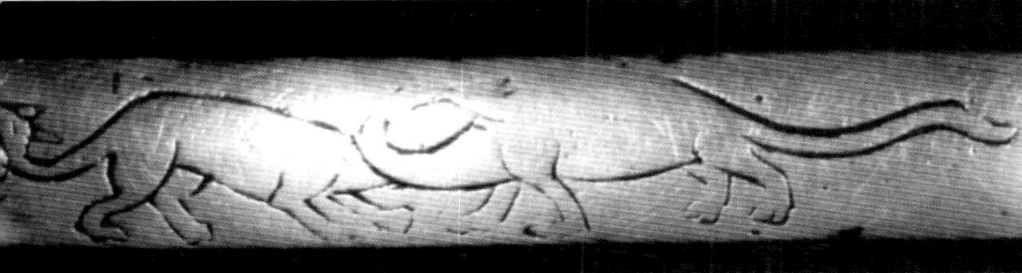

The tomb of Bishop Bell (died 1496) in Carlisle Cathedral has, engraved on the brass, pictures of fish, foliage, a hunting dog with collar but also dinosaurs with spikes on their tails. The tomb is now covered with a mat.

Giant fossil leaf

Evidently living conditions on earth have changed somewhat over time. There is geological evidence for an ice age a few thousand years ago. Neanderthal Man was affected by the lack of sunshine and the lack of fuel to make fire for cooking during this time. Rickets plagued them because of low levels of vitamin D. The facial bones were affected by the need for strong muscles to chew uncooked food. But they had human style ear labyrinths and larger brains than modern *H. sapiens*. Amazingly, they also lived for upwards of two hundred years, according to tests on Neanderthal teeth from Paris' Musée de l'Homme, carried out by orthodontist Jack Cuozzo. Cave paintings from this period are much too good to have won the Turner prize.

So the rocks tell us of rapidly deposited sedimentary rocks and rapidly erupted igneous rocks in the geological column on a young earth. Mountain building can be rapid according to the highly contorted sediments common in hilly regions. Rapid erosion has also been demonstrated, as on Surtsey. Oil and coal can be made quickly. The fossils give no comfort to evolutionists. They too can be formed quickly under bacterial action. There has been no change in their forms, just variation within a kind and devolution in size. There are no intermediate links.

The patriarch Job (12:8,9) told his friends to "speak to the earth, and it shall teach you ... that the hand of the LORD has wrought this". It does seem from observation that he was right.

CHAPTER 5

Design or chance?

Intelligent Design Movement

In the United States of America schoolchildren are not allowed to study creation science along with Darwinism. The country's constitution insists on the separation of church and state. The Discovery Institute was formed to get around this ban on religion in schools by presenting arguments for intelligent design (ID) in nature, without attempting to identify the Designer as God. Nature is replete with structures and mechanisms that seem to have been designed by an intelligent agent. In a test case in 2006 in Dover, Pennsilvania, a judge ruled that ID could not be taught in schools and universities. ID in the form of William Paley's *Natural Theology* was required reading in Oxford and Cambridge following its publication in 1802, and greatly impressed young Darwin. (Perhaps it is pertinent to note that some folk think the Americans also invented the modern creationist movement all of 30 years after the founding in The Strand, London in 1932 of the Evolution Protest Movement, since renamed the Creation Science Movement.)

One of the books on ID is Michael Behe's *Darwin's Black Box*. In it he argues that the complex molecular structures and mechanisms of living things were a mystery in Darwin's time, but many have now been elucidated. They have been found to be composed of lots of interdependent parts where nothing can work unless all the constituents are operational. He called this irreducible complexity. Such systems could not evolve a little at a time because they are of no use until complete. This opposes the thinking of Richard Dawkins in his *Climbing Mount Improbable*, where he says that a cliff can be ascended by taking the gentle path round the back in small steps, each stabilised by natural selection. A process of evolution by chance would have no predetermined goal, and each small step could only be established if it were an improvement.

One of Behe's examples is the process of blood clotting, that involves a cascade of complicated chemicals. Until such a system was working organisms with a blood circulation would be unable to survive an accidental cut. Another example is the cilia that rotate rapidly to move some bacteria around. The tiny motor has parts very like the system used to rotate the propeller of a boat, all made in miniature with proteins. These are illustrated and explained in Behe's excellent book.

> "Bacteria swim by rotating their helical flagella filaments. Each filament is driven with a flagellar motor embedded in the cell surface. The rotation rates of the motor had been reported to be high - we have observed rotation up to 1,700 rps. [revs per second] for polar flagellum of '*vibrio alginolyticus*'."
> Nature, 27th October 1994 p. 752

ATP Synthase and Kinosine are among a plethora of complex multi-component molecules found in every cell of all living systems, whether protozoa, fungi, plants or animals. Without ATP Synthase, food could not be converted into energy in the cell. ATP synthase is made of 31 enzymes, each precisely fashioned. It cannot work unless all are present and correct. No cell could function without these irreducibly complex motors.

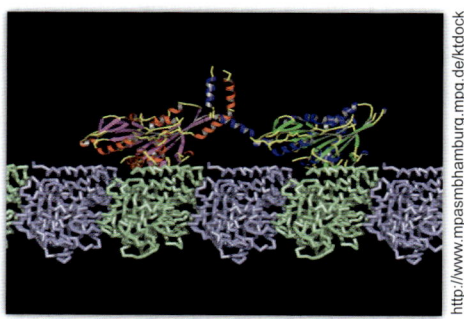

http://www.mpasmbhamburg.mpg.de/ktdock

Kinosine walking on a microtubule (diagrammatic).

Kinosine is also an ingenious molecule that delivers products from their point of manufacture along a network of microtubules to where they are to be used in the cell. It 'walks' along the tubules on two 'legs' that step out in planes at right angles to one another.

DNA, proteins and sugars

Not only do our bodies contain DNA and proteins that work together, but also a whole array of macromolecules known as polysaccharides. These sugars are each made up of more than 200 units linked together in a variety of ways. Their shapes enable them to perform specific tasks. Their functions in the body are vital. They are built by enzymes, which are proteins with a precise sequence of amino acids and a precise shape. In turn the proteins are coded for by genes that are also a precise sequence, in this case of nucleotides. The DNA, enzymes and sugars all constitute irreducibly complex systems. Some of these are described in *New Scientist* for 26th October 2002, starting on page 34.

In an earlier chapter we talked of the folding of proteins from a string of amino acids into a three dimensional shape, with active groups with the right geometry to enable them to engage in bio-chemical reactions. Water is squeezed out of the molecule as it folds so that van der Waals forces that can only attract over minute nano-distances hold the shape together. This elimination of water is accomplished with the help of a fairly simple chemical. For creatures that live in the depths of the sea, folding of proteins under high pressure is facilitated by the molecule trimethylamine oxide (TMAO). The deeper the habitat of the creature, the greater the concentration of TMAO in the cells. Unless this system were in place from the start, the proteins would not fold so the cells would not be able to operate. Natural selection could not help as the organism needs to reproduce for natural selection to have any offspring to select. This is mentioned in *New Scientist* for 11th December 1999 on page 10.

Another mechanism where natural selection cannot help because the process had to be operating from the beginning, is the protein that sticks cells together in an organism. The protein Claudin-1 is part of a structure known as 'tight junction' that holds cells together and controls the movement of water across layers of cells. Mice lacking this protein died within one day of birth by water loss through the skin. Claudin-1 is essential to all multi-cellular life, and must have been fully functioning from the beginning. This is discussed in *Nature Science Update* for 29th March 2002.

With our recently acquired ability to rapidly transcribe sequences of DNA, we are finding that genes in one organism are the same as the corresponding genes in some other organisms. The example is given of the reputed divergence of flies and frogs from a common ancestor: their analogous genes...

> "have diverged so little in more than half a billion years that scientists can snip the gene out of a fly, plug it into a frog, and it will work perfectly."
> New Scientist, 18th October 1997 p. 30

This has been explained as the result of the evolutionary process holding on to a system that works well. But this does not explain how the system arose in the first place. A common Designer seems a more reasonable explanation.

Eyes

Darwin admitted he felt sick when he considered the complexity of the eye and the beauty of the peacock's tail. Of course it is not just the eye we must consider but the optic nerve and the part of the brain that receives and make sense of the visual signals.

> "Light entering the eye changes the shape of a protein called retinal, triggering a chain of events that causes nervous impulses to be sent to the brain."
> New Scientist, 6th May 1995 p. 17

Design or chance?

One problem is how a humble creature on Darwin's tree of life, the fly, has an incredibly complex system for viewing its surroundings. The fly's compound eye is well suited to its needs. Flies have eyes that bristle with individual lenses, each looking at a small field of vision and each connected in parallel to its part of the brain that processes the information. This parallel system gives flies a response time 4 times faster than our own, as we soon discover when we try to swat one. As reported in *The Times* on 8th October 1993, computer designers are trying to imitate this idea with parallel processors. Designers of solar panels could also benefit from studying the eye of the humble fly.

> "Solar panels could be improved by mimicking the design of the eyes of a fly that lived 45 million years ago [according to the article]. A pattern of ridges found on the surface of the fly's eyes could reduce reflection and so allow panels to capture light arriving at very oblique angles."
> New Scientist, 17th April 1999 p. 21

The lobster is another creature considered by evolutionists to be low down on their tree of life. Its eye does not refract light. It channels the light through a kind of converging optical fibre bundle. This principle is being exploited to make an X-ray 'lens'. X-rays cannot be focussed like light. This is just one of many examples of where intelligent human designers are copying designs in nature that only work when all components are present.

The humble brittlestar has lenses that are a technological marvel. Arrays of minute calcite crystals focus light on to nerve bundles about 5 micrometers below them, such that the intensity of light on the photoreceptors is 50 times greater than at the surface of the lens.

> "The spindly arms of brittlestars may double as a primitive eye thanks to microscopic crystals in its skeleton that focus light. These tiny lenses rival the best that human technology can offer....It's astonishing that it's been able to build this essentially

out of coral."
New Scientist, 25th August 2001 p. 11

Moths have tiny eyes but they have colour vision, even at night.

"The moths use three separate colour receptors: blue, green and ultraviolet. At night that leaves so little light per receptor that the insects should be almost blind. But hawk moths have a host of adaptations to compensate. One is a mirror-like structure at the base of the eye, which reflects the light across the photoreceptors for a second time. The structure of the compound eye also allows each facet to supplement the light that strikes it with light from as many as 600 others."
New Scientist, 2nd November 2002 p. 23

The fish *Anableps anableps*, as reported in *New Scientist* for 6th December 2003 page 89, lives on the surface of the water and can focus on scenes both above and beneath the water. Fish normally have bulbous lenses to focus in water, whose refractive index is similar to that of the aqueous humour within the eye. The eyes of *A. anableps* have two pupils, one above and the other beneath the surface of the water mark. The eye is elliptical and the light from above encounters a smaller curvature than the underwater lens.

And how's this for a design feature:

There is now "evidence that molecules called cryptochromes in the birds' retinas, which undergo a chemical reaction that is sensitive to magnetic forces, allow the birds to literally see the magnetic field."
New Scientist, 13th November 2004 p. 20

Cats' eyes are slits that enable them to see clearly, not only in the dark, but also in bright sunshine.

"Slit pupils are found in species ranging from the Nile crocodile

to the domestic cat. They allow nocturnal animals to squint tightly in bright daylight to block out light that could harm their sensitive retinas... Such lenses have multiple concentric focal zones, each of which focuses different wavelengths into the retina. This means the eye can produce a sharply focused colour image even in low light conditions."
New Scientist, 7th January 2006 p. 14

Chameleons are not only able to rapidly change the colour of their skins to blend in with the background but uniquely the lenses of their eyes have a negative refractive index in order to magnify their insect prey as they stick their coiled, sticky tongue out at great speed to catch it. If the poor chameleon had had to wait for all these special features to evolve by chance it would have gone hungry.

"Chameleons are arboreal lizards that spot their prey visually and catch it by highly precise shots with their long sticky tongue ... Once an insect has been detected, the head axis is aligned towards the target, both eyes come forward to fixate the insect ... the sticky tongue is shot out with great precision. We have tested image magnification and find that it is higher than in any other vertebrate (scaled to the same size). This is a result of a unique optical design, unlike other vertebrate eyes, the lens of the chameleon has negative refractive power."
Nature, 23rd February 1995

Chameleon

Photo by Vij Sodera

Sometimes, particularly in older people, the lens of the eye becomes cloudy and a cataract operation must be performed to replace it with an artificial lens. The protein of our natural lens is designed to exacting specifications.

> "The lens of the eye presents an interesting biomechanical puzzle. Not only must it be transparent, to allow the passage of light and supply a refractive index gradient to avoid aberration, but its constituent materials must be highly stable to insult by ultraviolet light, radicals, and so on, because lens proteins cannot be regenerated."
> Nature, 6th October 1994 p. 538

If Charles Darwin had known as much as we now know about the various eyes found in the natural world, he would have had even more cause to feel queasy. Or maybe with such knowledge he would have given up on his theory. When evolutionists persist in their belief system, is it because their careers hang on its acceptance? Or could the theory be necessary so that they can deny the Intelligent Designer who commands repentance.

How do we smell?

The shape of volatile molecules may have a lock-and-key relationship with receptors in our noses that enable us to distinguish the smell of roses from lavender or whatever. There are about 1,000 olfactory receptor genes in the human genome. Of these, about 600 are described as pseudo-genes, many of which are functional in ethnically diverse people.

> "Humans can distinguish around 10,000 different smells via 400 receptor proteins lining the nasal cavity. But it has long been known that not everyone smells the same smells - and now geneticists have shown this could be because everyone has a different set of receptors.
> "They found that each person had a unique combination of

> functioning pseudo-genes, giving them an individualised
> repertoire of smell receptors."
> New Scientist, 31st January 2004 p. 40

The lifestyle of the rodent demands an even more acute sense of smell than our own. (Presumably they don't find sewers as repugnant as we do!)

> "Rats have an estimated 2,070 smell-receptor genes, about a third more than mice. As well as having more 'smell' genes than both us and mice, they have also evolved more genes that help detoxify chemicals."
> New Scientist, 3rd April 2004 p. 16

One has to wonder how they avoided the plague before these genes that help detoxify chemicals evolved.

The olfactory prowess of wasps and moths are not to be sniffed at.

> "The wasp can pick up scents at a concentration of one part in a thousand billion [10^{12}] - a hundred thousand times weaker than the lowest concentrations detected by commercial 'electronic noses'."
> New Scientist, 10th August 2002 p. 20

> "Is this the most sensitive nose on the planet? Male cotton leaf worm moths can detect the female's sex pheromone at a concentration of just five molecules in 10 millilitres of air … compares it to being able to detect that a sugar cube has been thrown into a medium-sized lake from one sip of the water… Minute amounts of pheromone were enough to trigger a jump in heart rate."
> New Scientist, 14th June 2003 p28

Nor are these abilities confined to animals and insects. The 28th September 1998 issue of *New Scientist* tells us that plants can also see, touch, smell, taste and hear. To discover which genes are responsible for these attributes, scientists can render a particular gene (of thale cress) inactive and see which properties are lost. One gene in the thale cress plant enables the roots to detect soil nutrients and grow towards them. An enzyme on the root surface tastes the soil for ATP (adenosine tri-phosphate) made by micro-organisms such as fungi. The plant converts ATP into vital phosphate nutrients.

Some plants such as corn, beet and cotton taste the saliva of caterpillars and send out volatile indoles and terpenes that attract wasps to lay eggs in the live caterpillars.

A wounded plant gives off methyl jasminate, a scent used in the perfume Chanel No. 5. Other plants smell this and produce the precursors of chemicals to repel insects or attract predators. (They just go on the alert rather than expending lots of energy making defence chemicals they may not use.) Buried tree seeds can detect the smell of smoke that triggers germination following a forest fire.

Climbing plants such as peas and beans coil round a support using a strong sense of touch. They sense prevailing winds and thicken stem tissue by summoning calcium ions to activate five genes. Mimosa and the Venus flytrap are well known for their sensitivity to touch.

The human voice has been used to double the growth of dwarf sweet peas by stimulating the production of the growth hormone gibberellic acid. Some gardeners indulge themselves by talking to the flowers, and now we know that it actually helps them to swell with pride!

Plants make proteins that attach themselves to light sensitive compounds and gather photons of light. Plants open up at different times of day, and respond to the length of the day.

The heliotropic properties of sunflowers shout design. At one stage in its development it follows the Sun through the day. However, once the pollen is formed it switches to simply facing East so that the pollen will not be damaged by noontide Summer temperatures. If it were possible for the first stage to evolve using a complex growth hormone, then until the change to the second stage evolved the pollen would fry and the flowers become extinct.

> "When the sunflower plant, *Helianthus annuus*, is in the bud stage, the head and the leaves do indeed track the path of the Sun...Interestingly, however, and contrary to popular belief, once the massive topmost flower opens into the radiance of yellow petals, it slows and then stops moving, ending up permanently facing east...Sunflower pollen gets damaged at temperatures greater than 30°C, so by facing east all the time, the flower reduces the net radiation falling on its face at noon, keeping itself cool and promoting fertilisation and seed development. In addition the heads receive more sunlight early in the morning, which helps dry off any dew...and decreases the likelihood of fungal attack. It also increases the temperature of the flower head in the chilly early morning, attracting warmth-loving insect pollinators."

Regarding the Sun-following mechanism of the first stage, we read:

> "The heliotropic movements of the leaves and sunflower bud are the result of bending during rapid growth. This is caused by build-up of the plant growth hormone auxine on the side of the stem opposite the Sun... When the Sun sets, the auxin is redistributed and the head swivels back, so that by around 3am it is facing east again, waiting for the Sun to come up."
> New Scientist, 3rd August 2002 p. 101

Spiders

Agur may not have known about the chemical and technological wizardry of spiders' webs, but he admits in Proverbs 30 that these little creatures are very clever and have access even to kings' palaces. The material inside the spider's body is a water soluble liquid which is extruded through a tapering duct to emerge as a water-resistant silk. The strands consist of 4 concentric tubes of different material with different properties. The one under the outer silk has fibres spiralling along it in both directions. The nano-fibres contain flat nano-crystals. The article that tells us these amazing facts adds:

"Spider silk is one of the strongest materials on earth."
New Scientist, 24th April 1999 p. 38

Spider web

Moreover:

"Spider silk is stronger than steel...Yet it can be stretched by more than one third and recover without distortion...Spiders' webs don't dissolve in the rain. That means that the protein is insoluble. But in the spider it starts by being secreted from a little gland into a bulbous sac. The sac's contents are liquid, so the protein must be soluble...Then it comes out as an insoluble solid."
New Scientist, 7th May 1994

and:

> "The web of the orb spider is mainly composed of two types of thread ... a framework of dry radial threads upon which is laid a single wet captive spiral."
> Nature, 12th January 1995 p. 146

> "David Knight of the University of Oxford and his colleagues tested strands of silk from the large orb-weaving spider *Nephila edulis* at temperatures between minus 60°C to 150°C. Knight found that over the entire temperature range the threads could stretch by at least 20 per cent before snapping."
> New Scientist, 22nd January 2005 p. 16

Beautiful Design

Beauty that goes beyond the requirements of utility is a hallmark of design rather than chance evolution. The tail of the peacock is over the top if we imagine that it evolved to attract the dull peahen.

> "The dazzling display of colour in a peacock's tail is produced by a surprisingly simple mechanism - a crystal structure woven into the bird's feathers…The team found that a lattice of melanin rods and keratin on the outer layer of each barbule forms a two-dimensional photonic crystal structure. The number and spacing of the rods determines the colour of the barbule and its intensity."
> New Scientist, 18th October 2003 p. 18

Similarly the delicate platelets of a butterfly's wings are specially designed so that it can separate the flapping wings against air pressure in flight. The colours involve refraction of light, with the serrations necessary for flight also enhancing the beauty.

> The bright colours on butterfly wings are produced by the finely serrated surface on minute platelets, refracting the light. The platelets also make it easier for the butterfly to flap its wings in flight. The platelets are hinged at one end and flap open as the

wings separate to ease the effect of the vacuum caused by the parting of the wings.
New Scientist, 17th July 1999

Nor is a butterfly just a pretty face:

"Butterflies may be nature's greatest chemists. German researchers have found that African milkweed butterflies can make more than 200 different chemicals, some never found in nature before."
New Scientist, 19th February 1994 p. 17

Designed sensing devices

Sight, smell, touch, hearing and taste are not the only probing senses found in nature. Sometimes a combination of devices is used as with the global migrations of birds, marine creatures and beasts. Some of these special senses are required where the distances involved preclude the use of sight alone.

"Honeybees are among the many organisms which can sense the earth's magnetic field through magneto-receptor cells [in the abdomen] ...Using a high-resolution transmission electron microscope, scientists have observed crystals of magnetite no more than 10 nanometres across at the core of some granules."
New Scientist, 23rd July 1994 p. 16

"The way the Jewel Beetle *Malanophila acuminata* homes in on forest fires from 20 miles away to lay eggs on charred wood, has been determined. The beetle has groups of 'sensilla' on its thorax which collect infra-red light from the fire. This is absorbed by a spherical organ within each sensillum, a mere hundredth of a millimetre across, which swells up, touching a nerve ending. This sensory system is thought to be unique. It converts infra-red light into heat to swell the sensilla, and thus into mechanical movement."
Nature, 24th April 1997 p. 773

NB. This is irreducible complexity.

Design or chance?

Bats emit squeaks of high frequency ultra-sound and map out their rapidly changing surroundings by analysing the echoes. Bat sonar is three times more precise than man-made sonar equipment. In a cave with thousands of bats, each can distinguish echoes from its own calls. Its ears close up in the fraction of a second it is squeaking and open again for the echo. Its batty brain processes the results rapidly to allow split second responses. Bats can distinguish between two objects the width of a pencil line apart with their sonar echo system. Squeaking at a particular frequency, listening for the echoes, processing the results and acting upon them is in total a programme of irreducible complexity. Even the comparatively crude man-made sonar was designed and engineered by very clever people. You can read all about it in the *Proceedings of the National Academy of Sciences* for October 1998.

In a thick swarm of bats, each one can distinguish its own squeaks from those of the host of others around it. When a bat chirps, it also closes its ears to avoid deafening itself and opens them again to hear the echo. That is a rapid mechanical response. When closing in on a moth, clicks become progressively fainter and more rapid in order to pin-point the moving target. The components of a bat's radar system are of no use unless the whole array is present, so it could not have evolved. The earliest fossil bat is just like today's bat. It was created complete with this complex direction-finding system.

The same ploy, but at much lower frequencies, is used by whales.

> "Whales have a cunning way of filtering the sound of their own 'voice' out of their echolocation systems, to help them navigate and locate prey. The clicks that whales produce for echolocation are loud, while the echoes that bounce back are faint."
> New Scientist, 7th June 2003 p. 26

While mentioning navigation, let us look just briefly at the navigational feats of some birds. They undertake prodigious journeys, sometimes without benefit of parental guidance.

Has Darwin had his day?

The *Daily Telegraph* on 13th January 1997 reported that a Common Tern has set a world record for the longest known flight by a bird: Ringed in Finland, it flew 16,000 miles to Victoria in south east Australia. The 4oz bird clocked up 125 miles a day for 18 weeks via the English Channel, the coasts of Europe and Africa.

And here's a trick they don't allow airline pilots to emulate:

> "Each year, migrating songbirds complete an epic journey, migrating thousands of kilometres to new wintering and breeding grounds. And even more startling, they do it with little, if any, sleep. How the birds manage to stay awake for so long is a mystery, but it doesn't appear to make them ill or impair their cognitive performance. This unparalleled ability also explains how migrating songbirds can fly through the night, while spending most of the day feeding to refuel."
> New Scientist, 17th July 2004 p. 10

Designer skin cream, sun block and nail care

There are some who need to buy skin care products, but the natural cream with which we were all coated at birth is better than all the manufactured products. A smear of vernix is made of 80% water, 10% lipids and 10% protein. When David says in Psalm 139 "Thou hast covered me in my mother's womb." he probably wasn't referring to vernix, but he might as well have been. It is exactly right to protect the unborn child.

> "The vernix that midwives wipe off before they hand the new mother her rosy-skinned bundle of joy is probably the best skin cream the baby will ever have. It has not only protected his or her skin from constant contact with water; it has kept it hydrated, its pH [acidity] balanced, and may even have primed it against infection and damage in preparation for birth."
> New Scientist, 17th January 2004 p. 40

Skin protection continues beyond birth with the colouration compound melanin. People whose families have lived in less sunny climates at high latitudes need to absorb all the vitamin D that is available through their skin. They are born with fair skin and fair hair and usually with blue eyes. People born to warmer climates are in danger of skin damage through too much sunlight, particularly ultraviolet light. These are born with brown or black skins and dark hair and eyes. Both types have melanin in their skins, but the black people have it in much greater concentration. The differences in the concentrations of melanin in the skins of people living at different latitudes balances out the need for vitamin D with the danger of skin cancer. While this state of affairs was probably arrived at through natural selection, the manufacture and distribution in the skin must have been designed.

"The natural tanning process results from our skin's love-hate relationship with sunlight. We need a certain level of UV radiation to allow keratinocytes, the main type of skin cells, to manufacture vitamin D, essential for healthy bones. But too much UV causes DNA mutations, which can lead to skin cancer. To balance these conflicting requirements, evolution has come up with a natural sunscreen called melanin. This is a light-absorbing pigment that is manufactured from the amino acid tyrosine in cells called melanocytes, in response to a substance called melanocyte-stimulating-hormone, or MSH. The cells release melanin from their long 'tentacles', and it disperses into surrounding keratinocytes.

"Perhaps surprisingly, it was only recently that scientists discovered how melanocytes detect that you have been in the sun. When UV rays damage the DNA in skin cells, repair enzymes excise short snippets of damaged DNA. In 1994 a team led by Barbara Gilcrest, a dermatologist at Boston University, showed   that these DNA snippets seem to make melanocytes more responsive to MSH, so they release more melanin. Her studies also suggested that the snippets trigger an array of protective systems against sun damage. 'Every time we look we find more pathways,' says Gilcrest."

New Scientist, 7th May 2005 p. 40

Has Darwin had his day?

Would an evolutionary process feel the need to throw up an array of protective systems rather than just one? Could a system involving the cooperation of DNA repair processes, tyrosine, the hormone MSH and melanin come together by chance? Yet this science reporter felt the need to repeat the mantra that 'evolution has come up with' a natural sunscreen.

Professor Susan Greenfield points out in the Independent on Sunday for 19th August 1997 that babies are similar to monkeys and apes in that the larynx is situated high in the throat so that it can form a seal over the airway. This permits food and drink to be consumed without fear of choking. Monkeys and apes grow up without changing in this respect. But with the human, at the age of about two, the larynx moves to a lower position, which in a baby would be dangerous if food went down the wrong way. The lower larynx enables the child to articulate a full range of sounds as it begins to speak. Monkeys and apes do not need this design feature since their brains are not equipped for speech.

We have all broken a nail from time to time. If the nail were to split along the axis of the finger and go down to the quick, it would be very painful for a long time while the nail grew back. However, you will have noticed that the nail tears across parallel to the finger tip. This is no accident. The nail is not a haphazard arrangement of keratin which would be strong but would tear in any direction. Nor is it simply layered to tear too readily in the safest way. It is a composite structure that defies an evolutionary 'just so' explanation.

> "Nails are made up of a sandwich of three layers of keratinous tissue. And Ennos's team found that it is the central layer - which has keratin fibres arranged parallel to the half-moon at the base of each nail - that prevents breaks from running down the nail rather than across it. And the randomly arranged keratin fibres in the two outer layers give each nail its bending strength."
> New Scientist, 7th February 2004 p. 19

Design or chance?

Our bones incorporate a means of fighting infection.

> "A study of infected and healthy pieces of jawbone, as well as healthy arm and hip bones revealed that the star-shaped cells called osteocytes, which are responsible for maintaining the strong calcium structures of bone, also churn out amino acid chains in response to infection." [The amino acid chains attack bacteria.]
> New Scientist, 19th November 2005 p. 19

Nor is the Intelligent Designer only concerned with mankind. His eye is on the sparrow also.

> "Calcutta sparrows may be taking natural remedies for malaria…While studying house sparrows, a team discovered all their nests had been thickly lined with the quinine-rich leaves of the krishnatura tree, *Caesalpinia pulcherrima*...Calcutta sparrows used to line their nests with the leaves of the neem tree…the switch to Caesalpinia leaves coincided with a malaria outbreak, and argues that the birds ingest them to kill the malaria parasite.
> New Scientist, 3rd January 1998 p. 19

> "Birds that collect aromatic leaves for lining their nests are not just indulging in feng shui. It seems the plants kill off microbes that destroy proteins in their feathers."
> New Scientist, 15th June 2004 p. 16

And the penguin.

> "Male king penguins store undigested food in their stomachs for up to three weeks, a talent unique among higher vertebrates. This ensures a constant supply of food for their chicks. Now an analysis of the birds' stomach contents shows the penguins keep food fresh by destroying bacteria in their stomachs, suggesting that they produce an antibacterial agent in their digestive tracts.

But the birds appear to be able to switch on the preservation process, suggesting that they actively release one or more bactericidal agents."
New Scientist, 22nd February 2003 p. 21

And Kanga and baby Roo.

Ben Cocks of Melbourne "has found that [marsupial] mother's milk contains a molecule that is 100 times more effective against Gram-negative bacteria such as E. coli than the most potent form of penicillin. The molecule, called AGG01, also kills four types of Gram-positive bacteria and one type of fungus."
Marsupial foetuses in the mother's pouch lack their own immune system.
New Scientist, 22nd April 2006 p. 16

Optical fibres are carefully designed, but sponges do it better. It is not that sponges are particularly clever. But the Intelligent Designer is.

"And Lucent Technologies' Bell Laboratories is trying to work out how deep-sea sponges manage to grow glass skeletons at low temperatures that are both tougher and better at transmitting light than optical fibres."
New Scientist, 12th November 2005 p. 36

King penguins
Painting by Lisa Sodera

CHAPTER 6

Sinking Sands or Solid Rock

The fundamentals

In spite of the foregoing evidence, the rumour persists that Evolution is science and that Creation is nonsense. The vehemence of the invective against creationism suggests that the objection to 'religion' is emotional rather than scientific. Some scientists believe in evolution theory in spite of, rather than because of, the evidence of experiment and observation.

> 'We take the side of science in spite of the patent absurdity of some of its constructs, in spite of its failure to fulfil many of its extravagant promises of health and life, in spite of the tolerance of the scientific community for unsubstantiated just-so stories, because we have a prior commitment, a commitment to materialism. It is not that the methods and institutions of science somehow compel us to accept a material explanation of the phenomenal world, but, on the contrary, that we are forced by our *a priori* adherence to material causes to create an apparatus of investigation and a set of concepts that produce material explanations, no matter how counter-intuitive, no matter how mystifying to the uninitiated. Moreover, that materialism is an absolute, for we cannot allow a Divine Foot in the door.'
>
> Richard Lewontin, Billions and billions of demons, The New York Review, 9th January 1997 p. 31

Lewontin is a fundamentalist evolutionist. Others, such as Professor Lipson of Manchester are willing to consider the evidence.

> "I think, however, that we must go further and admit that the only acceptable explanation is creation. I know that this is anathema to physicists, as indeed it is to me, but we must not

reject a theory we do not like if the experimental evidence supports it."
Prof. H J Lipson, A Physicist looks at Evolution, Physics Bulletin, vol.31, 1980, p.138

In the foregoing chapters we have pointed out the shortcomings of evolutionism in astronomy, geology, genetics and biology. We have argued that where there is indubitable evidence of design we must invoke a Designer. Yet as arguments mount up, the evolutionists become ever more shrill in their condemnation of creation science and intelligent design. Christian creationists are accused of promoting Christian values, as though that were a crime.

"In the US, Christian fundamentalists seek to change the abortion laws, promote sexual abstinence, ban gay marriage, force doctors to keep terminally ill people alive against their wishes and impose the teaching of creationism."
New Scientist, 8th October 2005 p. 39

Fundamentalists are those who believe in the fundamentals of the faith, but today it is used as a term of abuse. Religion is seen as the reason behind wars, and the Crusades of the politically powerful medieval church are regularly cited to support this idea. Never mind that such aggression is quite contrary to the teaching of Jesus Christ.

"The problem is not necessarily religious fundamentalism so much as intolerance. The bottom line is that most of the millions massacred in the 20th century were murdered not by religious fanatics but by adherents of the secular faiths of fascism, Marxist-Leninism, nationalism."
New Scientist, 5th November 2005 p. 20

and

"The leader of Germany [Adolph Hitler] is an evolutionist, not only in theory, but, as millions know to their cost, in the rigour

of its practice. For him, the national front of Germany is also the evolutionary front."
Essays in human evolution by Sir Arthur Keith, FRS, written in 1942.

Hospitals, schools, relief agencies and charities started out for the most part as Christian initiatives.

Rejoice!

There is a case to be made that we are putting the fun into fundamentalism. Apparently recent sociological studies confirm this.

> "Recent sociological studies have shown that compared with non-religious people, the actively religious are happier, live longer, suffer fewer physical and mental illnesses, and recover faster from medical interventions such as surgery… Endorphins flood the brain, creating a mild 'high'. Perhaps that is why religious people often seem so happy."
> New Scientist, 28th January 2006 p. 28

Of course, if as an evolutionist you find no purpose in life, and you can only look forward to old age and death as required by the second law of thermodynamics (change and decay), then you will not be surprised by joy very often. Two of Britain's more eminent and outspoken anti-creationists are Oxford Professors Peter Atkins and Richard Dawkins. The latter quotes his mournful colleague in one of his evolution-promoting books.

> We are children of chaos, and the deep structure of change is decay. At root, there is only corruption, and the unstemmable tide of chaos. Gone is purpose; all that is left is direction. This is the bleakness we have to accept as we peer deeply and dispassionately into the heart of the Universe.
> Peter Atkins, quoted by Richard Dawkins: Unweaving the Rainbow, p. ix

Significantly, it is not only the fundamentalists who experience *joie de vivre*.

Sinking Sands or Solid Rock?

The whole of Creation seems to enjoy a good frolic.

> "Have you ever watched jackdaws on a windy day? Instead of clinging to a perch and waiting for the whirling weather to pass, they get out and ride a Ferris wheel of air with scarcely a flap, just a subtle shaping and reshaping of the wing. There is no survival advantage conveyed by this behaviour: no food, no territory, no mate to win, no rival to be vanquished. It seems they ride the wind for the same reason that humans go surfing. Horses gallop about a field because it's a nice day. A seagull glides the eddies and updraughts along a cliff edge for no apparent reason other than the love of flight. And a bird sings - well, it sounds an awful lot as if the pure love of singing has something to do with it."
>
> New Scientist, 18th June 2005 p. 51

Theistic evolutionists

Within some twenty years of the publication of Charles Darwin's *On the origin of species* many within the Christian church had capitulated to the findings of 'Science'. Although the majority of evolutionists do not want to countenance the case for a Deity, many Christian scientists and laymen compromise by saying that God used evolution to produce the world as we know it. They say that the early chapters of Genesis were written by primitive people copying the stories of Sumerians and Egyptians. They explain away the miracles. The global Flood was probably the folk memories of many local floods world-wide. The Resurrection and the Second Coming are spiritualised. They then complain that fundamentalists are turning folk - who don't want to be regarded as unsophisticated or unscientific - away from joining the church. The praises of men and the wisdom of this world are more important to them.

However, there are many well qualified scientists who have no faith in the theory of evolution. They are neither unsophisticated nor unscientific. Here are some examples of their thoughts about the subject:

Has Darwin had his day?

Dr. Michael Denton, who holds three earned doctorates, MD, PhD and DSc writes:

> "The hold of the evolutionary paradigm is so powerful that an idea which is more like a principle of medieval astrology than a serious twentieth century scientific theory has become a reality for evolutionary biologists."
> Evolution: a theory in crisis p. 306

On the final page Denton says:

> "Ultimately the Darwinian theory of evolution is no more nor less than the great cosmogenic myth of the twentieth century."

Dr. T N Tahmisian, Director, US Atomic Energy Commission has written:

> "Scientists who go about teaching that evolution is a scientific fact are great con-men and the story they tell is the greatest hoax ever. They do not have one iota of fact."

Steven Rose wrote in the *New Scientist*, 24th January 1998 p. 42:

> "Evolutionary stories are, almost by definition, Just So stories, like Rudyard Kipling's explanation of how the elephant got its trunk."

On 7th August 1999, *New Scientist* reported:

> At this point there is a serious risk that we are making up plain 'Just So stories'. It is both a weakness and a strength of evolutionary theories that they can explain almost anything: testing theories is a lot more difficult."

In the *New Scientist*, 22nd April 2000 p. 32, Bryan Appleyard, author & *Sunday Times* journalist, wrote:

"A theory that explains everything might just as well be discarded since it plainly has no real explanatory value. The other thing about evolution is that anything can be said because very little can be disproved."

One could multiply such quotations many-fold. If one says that God used evolution, just so that one may follow the crowd, then yes, one is clearly "unsophisticated and unscientific".

As to being scientific, followers of evolution theory cannot even agree on the mechanisms of evolution - big bang or steady state; gradualism or punctuated equilibrium; uniformitarianism or catastophism.

Various former evidences have been dropped as our knowledge has become more complete - vestigial organs, embryonic recapitulation, Piltdown Man, Nebraska Man, horse evolution, peppered moths. The evolutionists' science needs to be continually revised.

The theory is undermined by unproven hypotheses - origin of life, missing links, origin of whales, and so on.

Some atheistic evolutionists can see the untenable, illogical position of theistic evolutionists very clearly. 'Darwin's bulldog', Thomas Henry Huxley wrote as follows:

"I am fairly at a loss to comprehend how anyone, for a moment, can doubt that Christian theology must stand or fall with the historical trustworthiness of the Jewish Scriptures. The very conception of the Messiah, or Christ, is inextricably interwoven with Jewish history; the identification of Jesus of Nazareth with that Messiah rests upon the interpretation of passages of the Hebrew Scriptures which have no evidential value unless they possess the historical character assigned to them, If the covenant with Abraham was not made; if circumcision and sacrifices were not ordained by Jahveh; if the 'ten words' were not written by God's hand on the stone tables; if Abraham was more or less a

mythical hero, such as Theseus; the story of the Deluge a fiction; that of the Fall a legend; and that of the Creation the dream of a seer; … if all these definite and detailed narratives of apparently real events have no more value than have the stories of the regal period of Rome - what is to be said about the Messianic doctrine, which is so much less clearly enunciated? And what about the authority of the writers of the books of the New Testament, who, on this theory, have not merely accepted flimsy fictions for solid truths, but have built the very foundations of Christian dogma upon legendary quicksands?"
T. H. Huxley, Science and Hebrew Tradition, Macmillan & Co, 1901

Huxley was, of course, quite sure that the Old Testament was full of legends and that the Messiah, the Lord Jesus Christ, was not the Creator. He wrote to undermine Christianity and show that if its doctrines and Scriptures were false then theistic evolutionists should come down off the fence in favour of atheistic evolutionism. Another atheist who wrote along similar lines was G. Richard Bozarth.

"Christianity has fought, still fights and will fight science to the desperate end over evolution, because evolution destroys utterly and finally the very reason Jesus' earthly life was supposedly made necessary. Destroy Adam and Eve and the original sin, and in the rubble you will find the sorry remains of the son of God. Take away the meaning of his death. If Jesus was not the redeemer who died for our sins, and this is what evolution means, then Christianity is nothing! …What all this means is that Christianity cannot lose the Genesis account of creation … and get along. The battle must be waged, for Christianity is fighting for its very life."
G. Richard Bozarth, American Atheist, February 1978 p. 30

Would that the theistic evolutionists who compromise the truth of Scripture in the Church today could borrow the spectacles of men like Huxley and Bozarth. It is liberating to know that *all* Scripture is given by inspiration of God. As Jesus said, "Thy Word is truth". Psalm 119 specifically says "Thy Word is true from the beginning".

Ethics and evolution theory

Following the break-up of the Soviet Union the Russian president Boris Yeltsin called a conference to celebrate two thousand years of Christianity. The conference in Moscow's National Academy of Education, at which I was among those invited to speak, addressed the problem of what should be the basis for ethics now that the state religion of communism had lost its authority. The Russian Orthodox Church delegates, together with some invited Americans (and me for the UK!), concluded that the best basis for ethics was, in fact, the 'ten words' derided by Huxley. Written by the finger of God, they include the claim that in six days the Lord made heaven and earth. Incidentally, the President of the Russian National Academy of Education, a Christian creationist, heartily agreed with the conclusion of the conference that the Ten Commandments should be taught in Russian schools.

If everything came about by chance there can be no standard of right or wrong, good or bad. This is lawlessness. Might is right, the survival of the fittest. Selfishness rules and society collapses. Without God's rules, why should anyone agree to honour their parents, agree not to murder, commit adultery, steal, lie or covet.

If man is not made in the image of God (Genesis 9:6), human life is not sacrosanct. If man is no more than an evolved primate, then life is cheap. Ethnic cleansing becomes a matter of economics rather than morality. The most vulnerable are the very old and the very young. The organisation EXIT regularly brings test cases for euthanasia. If it is permitted by law for a consenting sick old person, this opens the way down a slippery slope to involuntary euthanasia The old and sick will fear to go into hospital, and will mistrust their heirs. Some may even feel that it is their duty to shuffle off this mortal coil before they're pushed.

Has Darwin had his day?

There has been an outcry recently when it came to light that greyhounds were being put down once their racing days were over. On what moral grounds would an evolutionist regard retired humans as in a different category from greyhounds? Once he had himself retired he would indeed find some good reason!

Was the Good Samaritan illogical to help the less fit? And what about famine relief? Do Aid programmes exacerbate the problems of limited world resources? Why not let nature take its toll, if man is not special? This is not to say that individual evolutionists are uncaring; but helping the less fit to survive is not a logical corollary of the theory of evolution.

Perhaps most vulnerable are the unborn. A mother's womb should be the safest place on earth, but since the passing of the abortion act in 1968 six million embryos have been aborted in the UK. There have been arguments about when an embryo becomes a person. Thanks to advances in genetics, we now know that it is at conception.

"The task force finds that the new recombinant DNA technologies indisputably prove that the unborn child is a whole human being from the moment of fertilisation, that all abortions terminate the life of a living human being, and that the unborn child is a separate human patient under the care of modern medicine.

"The task force cited scientific advances since 1973 as showing an embryo to be a 'whole, separate, unique, living, human being' from the moment of conception. The advances in question included DNA fingerprinting, which shows a pattern of DNA that can identify an individual, and the polymerase chain reaction, which makes it possible to amplify and extract that information from a single cell... The task force also cited findings that control of growth and development are established by the embryo's DNA after the third division of the fertilised egg: this stage is reached long before the embryo is implanted in the womb, which has previously been cited as when parenthood began."

Sinking Sands or Solid Rock?

"Several large studies suggest that women are more likely to suffer from depression, bipolar disorder, and suicidal thoughts following an abortion and are more likely to abuse drugs."
New Scientist, 18th March 2006 p. 8

When people contend that abortion should be permitted because a woman has a right to control her own body, that argument is no longer valid. The embryo's body is genetically separate. It is an individual in its own right from conception. Of course a mother must be concerned for the well-being of her own body. In fact she needs to protect herself from the dangers of depression, bipolar disorder, suicidal tendencies and drug abuse!

The arguments for making abortion freely available are the health risk for the mother, and the danger that the child will have a debilitating or fatal condition. These were prominent discussion points in David Steel's 1968 bill. However the official statistics published by The Stationery Office for 1996 were as follows:
Precisely three abortions out of a total of 167,916 for residents in England and Wales during 1996 were carried out on the grounds that it was immediately necessary to save the life of the pregnant woman or prevent grave permanent injury to the physical or mental health of the pregnant woman.

This figure of 3 may be compared with the 57 cases of sepsis, 226 of haemorrhage, 131 of perforation, 120 unspecified complications as a direct result of legal abortions. As we saw from the quotation above, a woman's health is much more likely to suffer from having an abortion than from not having one. How strange that the stigma of having an illegitimate child can be greater than that of murdering your own vulnerable unborn child.

If man is not thought of as made in the image of his Maker, our ideas can be turned on their head. Human babies can be culled as easily as seal pups. Though in neither case is the process painless.

Francis Galton, a cousin of Darwin, invented the pseudo-science of Eugenics. This was an attempt to breed out undesirable traits from the human stock. People with severe physical and mental conditions were sterilised to prevent them passing on defective genes. By 1935 sterilisation laws had been passed in several European countries and in the USA, affecting the physically, mentally and morally defective. Hitler used these ideas in his attempt to breed a pure Aryan race. He also carried out an ultimate solution to the problem he had with Jews and Gypsies.

Related to these ideas was a suggestion to set up a sperm bank for particularly talented and healthy males, along the lines of Hitler's pure race of blonde, blue eyed Aryans. The story is told of the actress who wrote to the playwright George Bernard Shaw suggesting that he sire her baby. "With your brains and my looks the child would have a head start in life". GBS is said to have responded: "Madam, supposing it had your brains and my looks!"

If man and woman were not made in the image of God and told to be fruitful and multiply, then biblical family values are not applicable. There could then be no logical objection to the anti-scriptural arrangements of casual relationships, polygamy or even same-sex partnerships. Eve was made from the side of Adam, so the two were one flesh. The Creator, the Lord Jesus Christ, referred to this when asked about divorce. (Matt, 19: 5). Paul tells us that this is a picture of Christ and the Church (Eph. 5: 32). Christ goes on to say "What therefore God has joined together let not man put asunder (Mal. 2:16). Broken homes damage the children. Permanent marriages were the Creator's Plan A from the beginning.

If man came down out of the trees millions of years ago, lost his opposable big toes and his body hair, adjusted his pelvis and his ear labyrinths, grew a big brain and lost much of his muscular power, then some tribes would be more advanced than others. Darwin, Huxley and Haeckel were white supremacists, believing that the coloured races were less highly evolved than the Europeans. Racism was already rife, with the slaves not long emancipated in the West and apartheid still practised well into the twentieth century in some lands. Creationists know that Eve was the mother of all living, and genetic studies confirm this. Paul told his listeners at Athens that we are all one big family (Acts 17:26).

Yes, racism is practised by some Christians, but it is contrary to biblical teaching. I recall that on one of our many visits to St. Andrews University in Scotland, a group of coloured students came to us after the presentation. They wanted us to confirm that all races are descendants of Adam and Eve. They left on cloud 9. Something we take as fundamental had not been part of their education prior to coming to the UK.

I have saved my biggest argument against theistic evolution until last. If evolution theory is true, sin has no meaning. If there were no Fall, if we did not all die in Adam, we are not fallen sinners and do not need a Saviour. This is what G. Richard Bozarth saw so clearly. If there was no original fall from a perfect Creation, then there can be no re-creation in Christ. 'For as in Adam all die, even so in Christ shall all be made alive.' (I Cor. 15:22). Adam was told that his disobedience would bring death. 'The wages of sin is death' (Rom. 6:23). 'Sin came by one man, and death through sin' (Rom. 5:12). Evolution theory would say that there were hundreds of millions of years of death before man eventually evolved a conscience telling him he had ever done anything wrong.

Theistic evolutionists should note that if our first parents were not disobedient, incurring physical death and separation from their Creator, then Jesus Christ did not need to become accursed for us. The shedding of His blood, His physical death and being forsaken by God at the cross, would not be for the remission of man's sins. As Bozarth has rightly pointed out: "Destroy Adam and Eve and the original sin, and in the rubble you will find the sorry remains of the son of god".

Does one really want a god who lit the blue touch paper of the big bang and retired immediately, leaving mutations and natural selection to somehow bring us to where we are today? Or do we want the hands-on God of the Bible who made His plan of salvation before He spoke the world into being - "The Lamb slain from the foundation of the world"?

Barracuda shoal

You have been surprised? That is to be expected. This book has given you the information on evolution theory gleaned from the scientists' camp. Evolutionist scientists themselves let drop that this evolutionary bulwark is flawed, and that its arguments do not stand up to examination. Every statement on evolution is found to be on a slippery slope when checked out. Not what you are led to believe from the media, encyclopaedia and textbooks.

So it turns out that there must be a Designer/Creator. Those first chapters of Genesis are right, and so you can trust the rest of the Bible too. And in turn, our children can be taught a sound basis for right and wrong.

There has to be wrong, otherwise we would have been made like automatons with no free will. And wrong has to be dealt with. The good news starts right there in the third chapter of Genesis where God promises to come as the Seed of the woman, and He would defeat Satan by paying with His own life for the wrong. Trace the story as it unfolds - the promise renewed to Abraham, to David, to Mary. All those prophecies were fulfilled in the smallest detail, finishing with the resounding promise, yet to come, of His return to reign.

You hate it when someone pulls a fast one on you? So do we all. But that is what the education system and media are doing to you right now. Glance back through the arguments you found most telling in this little book - it is time for action. Join the thousands of people worldwide, qualified scientists and that 'man on the Clapham omnibus', who have signed up to receive quarterly mailings from the CSM (Creation Science Movement, founded in 1932). Subscribers pay £10 for UK membership, £12 overseas - not enough to break the bank. Many of the telling quotations from the New Scientist and other journals that you have read in this book were previously quoted in the CSM journal

Creation. You get the latest ideas and developments without having to trawl through the science publications yourself. And along with the journal you get a new pamphlet every quarter giving you the basic facts on some aspect of Creation, in language you can understand. (None of us is a specialist in every field.)

Send to CSM, PO Box 888, Portsmouth PO6 2YD, UK.

See our website www.csm.org.uk with its secure shop for books, DVDs, pamphlets and subscriptions.

Visit the UK's only permanent creationist exhibition, the Genesis Expo (entrance free) right by the Historic Dockyard at 17-18 The Hard, Portsmouth PO1 3DT in the heart of the tourist area.

Best of all, know that you now have reasons for believing that 'In the beginning God created the heavens and the earth'. Your week-end break is part of the story! Creation took the Lord God as long as six days - why? Exodus 20 will tell you. So He really is all-powerful, and He paid a massive ransom for you.

Damaris Curtis BA, Dip. Ed.

INDEX

ABOUT THE AUTHOR
David Rosevear, PhD, FRSC, CChem

Photo by Vij Sodera

Joan and David snapped

David Rosevear became a Christian while in his teens. He married Joan in 1954 and they have three sons and three grandchildren to date. Having graduated in Chemistry and worked for eight years in the head office research laboratories of Imperial Chemical Industries, he was invited by Professor F G A Stone, FRS to research for a doctoral degree at the University of Bristol. For the next two decades he lectured at Portsmouth Polytechnic, now the University of Portsmouth, and has published a score of papers in secular scientific journals. He took early retirement in the late eighties as pressure to do more lecturing and debating on Creation built up. He had joined the Council of the Creation Science Movement in the mid seventies and became its Chairman in 1985. (CSM is the world's oldest creationist organisation, having been founded in 1932.)

David has lectured on Creation and Evolution Theory throughout the UK as well as in a dozen other countries from Los Angeles to Moscow. He has lectured and debated in twenty-three universities, many with several repeat visits. He is asked for interviews in newspapers, radio and television as public interest in the topic of Creation has increased.

One of his books, 'Creation Science, confirming that the Bible is right' has been reprinted as well as being translated into Czech and Russian. He designed and supervised the building of the UK's only permanent creationist exhibition, the Genesis Expo, just by Portsmouth's Historic Dockyard that is always teeming with tourists from around the globe. Since its opening in 2000 the Genesis Expo has hosted many tens of thousands of visitors.

The Genesis Expo

Photo by Vij Sodera

SUGGESTED READING

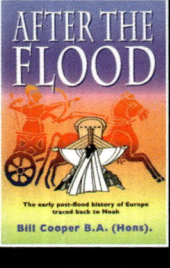

After the Flood
Bill Cooper £7.95

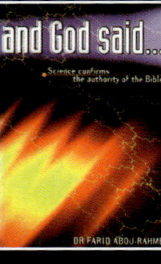

And God Said
Farid Abou-Rhame £

...ng of Chinese Characters
...Broadberry & Wang £9.50

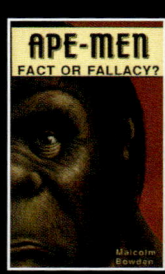

Ape-Men: Fact or Fa...
Malcolm Bowden £

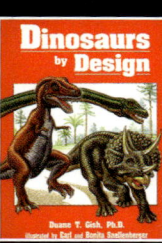

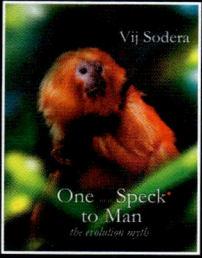

One Small Speck* to Man
Vij Sodera £32.00

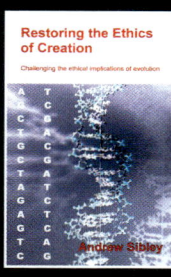

Restoring the Ethics of Creation
Andrew Sibley £12.50

Science versus Evolution
Malcolm Bowden £7.95

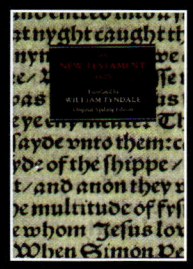

William Tyndale's 1526 New Testament Ed.
Bill Cooper £14.95

Paley's Watchmaker
Bill Cooper £7.95

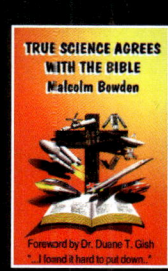

Rise of the Evolution Fraud
Malcolm Bowden £5.95

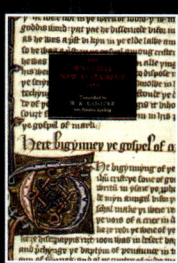

True science agrees with the bible
Malcolm Bowden £10.95

Wycliffe New Testament 1388, Ed.
Bill Cooper £20.00

A selection of displays from the Genesis Expo
17-18 The Hard, Portsmouth, PO1 3DT